Instructor's Manual to Accompany

CORRECTIONS
A Concise Introduction

James F. Quinn
University of North Texas

WAVELAND

PRESS, INC.

Prospect Heights, Illinois

For information about this book, write or call:
  Waveland Press, Inc.
  P.O. Box 400
  Prospect Heights, Illinois 60070
  (847) 634-0081

Printed in the United States of America

7 6 5 4 3 2 1

Contents

Chapter One

The Goals of Correctional Policy

Learning Objectives

1. Explain the relationship between corrections and each of the three branches of government with emphasis on how various political agendas affect system problems and policies.
2. Differentiate between "punishment" and "discipline" as they relate to attempts to change behavior.
3. Define the basic goals that may be assigned to correctional systems and discuss the assumptions made by each.
4. Relate the methods used to sentence offenders to (a) basic models of criminal justice and (b) the main justifications of punishment recognized by our society.
5. Describe the effects of new sentencing laws on corrections, crime rates, and the overall welfare of society.
6. Discuss why all of the goals of corrections cannot be simultaneously met by any program or policy.

Chapter Outline

The Political Context of Corrections
Defining Modern Correctional Goals
    Punishment, Discipline, and Behavior Change
Moral and Utilitarian Views of the Correctional Mission
    Retribution
    Restitution
    Deterrence
    Setting Social Boundaries
    Incapacitation
     Habitual Offenders and the Prediction Problem
    Treatment-reintegration
Correctional Decision-making

1

Major Points

1. The goals, resources, and policies of correctional agencies are determined by political institutions that are more sensitive to public opinion than to science.

2. The mere infliction of pain is unlikely to alter behavior patterns in a positive manner but may be useful in achieving what many define as "justice."

3. Retribution, rehabilitation-reintegration, deterrence, and incapacitation have been the principle goals of corrections at different points in U.S. history, but restitution and boundary-setting must also be acknowledged as worthy correctional goals.

4. The legal approach to corrections focuses on the nature and frequency of the illegal act(s) and seeks to assure equality and justice. The scientific approach is oriented to efficient control of crime and its costs; it stresses the uniqueness of each offender as it relates to the need for incapacitation, treatment, and prevention.

5. Most states rely heavily on indeterminate sentencing which empowers parole boards or prison authorities and is based on the scientific model of corrections. Newer, more popular sentencing methods, such as three strikes laws and mandatory and presumptive sentencing, are based on the legal model and seek mainly to incapacitate and punish.

6. The conflicts between justice and efficiency as well as between rehabilitation-reintegration and punishment (incapacitation, deterrence, and retribution) can never be fully reconciled because their foci and assumptions are so different.

Key Terms

Boundary-setting
Community service
Determinate sentences
Deterrence
Good time laws
Habitual offender laws
Incapacitation
Indeterminate sentences
Just deserts
Legal model
Life-without-parole
Mandatory sentences
Presumptive sentences

Preventive detention
Principle of least eligibility
Rate of incarceration
Reintegration
Restitution
Retribution
Scientific model
Sentence enhancement
Sentencing guidelines
Social control
Three strikes laws
Truth-in-sentencing
Utilitarian arguments

Chapter Highlights

This chapter describes the social and political context in which correctional policies and practices develop and contrasts the idea of punishment with the factors that promote self-discipline and positive behavior change. Most of the chapter is devoted to a discussion of the moral and utilitarian rationales for criminal punishment and the methods by which they are implemented as policy. The assumptions that underlie retribution, incapacitation, deterrence, restitution, and treatment-reintegration are described and the limitations of each is noted. Classical-legal and scientific-positive approaches to the question of crime control are introduced and provide a general structure for the chapter. Discussion of the methods by which offenders are sentenced today—indeterminate, determinate, mandatory, and presumptive—is woven into this overview. The idea that each of these structures empowers a different part of government (i.e., parole board, judge, legislature, sentencing commission) to set criminal penalties is pivotal to these changes. Recent innovations in sentencing such as three strikes laws and truth-in-sentencing are compared with habitual offender laws and the problem of predicting which offenders will recidivate is introduced.The economic effects of harsh sentencing practices are reviewed and trends in U.S. imprisonment rates are briefly outlined.

Examination Questions

Multiple Choice Items

1. The study of corrections focuses on:
   a. criminals.
   b. prisons.
   c. probation/parole agencies.
   d. agency employees.
   e. all of the above.*

2. Which of the following is most likely to result in a law-abiding lifestyle?
   a. punishment
   b. discipline*
   c. unconditional positive regard
   d. all of the above

3. _____ are/is the central goal(s) of modern corrections.
   a. Fair punishment and social control
   b. Efficient crime control
   c. Both of the above*
   d. Neither of the above

4. The philosophy of punishment that emphasizes the relief of guilt through penance is called:
   a. deterrence.
   b. expiation.*
   c. restitution.
   d. retribution.

5. _____ seeks to prevent or discourage crime through swift, certain, and appropriately severe punishment.
   a. Deterrence*
   b. Expiation
   c. Restitution
   d. Retribution

6. _____ deterrence attempts to make an example of known offenders so as to reduce the likelihood and rate of undesirable behavior in the general population.
   a. General*
   b. Specific
   c. Exemplar
   d. Restitutive

7. _____ deterrence punishes an offender to discourage that person from repeating the crime.
   a. General
   b. Specific*
   c. Exemplar
   d. Restitutive

8. Attempts to morally equalize the wrong done by an offense by allowing, and even advertising, vengeance against the offender are justified by the concept of:
   a. deterrence.
   b. expiation.
   c. restitution.
   d. retribution.*

9. Changing an offender into a person who can lead a productive life in conventional society is called:
   a. deterrence.
   b. incapacitation.
   c. rehabilitation.*
   d. retribution.

10. _____ arguments for punishment focus on the practical goal of reducing crime as much as possible while spending as little as possible on criminal justice.
   a. Utilitarian*
   b. Legal
   c. Moral
   d. Medical

11. _____ arguments for punishment focus on the search for justice and the role of the justice process in righting the wrongs done by offenders.
   a. Utilitarian
   b. Legal
   c. Moral*
   d. Medical

12. The origins of the _____ model are usually traced to the positive school of criminology which tries to identify and treat the causes of crime.
   a. scientific*
   b. justice
   c. reciprocal
   d. spurious

13. The scientific model of criminal sentencing tends to focus its attention on the:
    a. criminal offense.
    b. offender.*
    c. offender's biology.
    d. politics of sentencing.

14. The scientific approach infers that some form of _____ is guiding the behavior of the offender.
    a. conscious choice
    b. supernatural entity
    c. determinism*
    d. mental illness

15. The scientific approach to corrections often presumes that _____ has contributed to the offender's behavior problems in some way and is therefore morally obligated to help in solving the offender's problems.
    a. the family
    b. biology
    c. the media
    d. society*

16. Retribution is closely related to the doctrine of _____ , or an eye for an eye, a tooth for a tooth.
    a. *mens rea*
    b. *lex talionis**
    c. *actus reas*
    d. *corpus delicti*

17. Both deterrence and retribution assume that:
    a. most criminals will be quickly caught and punished.
    b. crime results from a rational calculation of the costs and benefits of various actions.
    c. the reward value of crime can be affected by legal penalties.
    d. all of the above.*

18. Restitution is unique among the philosophies of punishment due to its emphasis on the welfare of the:
    a. offender.
    b. victim.*
    c. government.
    d. justice process.

19. "You must die, not because you have killed, but in order to teach others not to kill" is an example of which of the following justifications of punishment?
    a. restitution
    b. general deterrence*
    c. retribution
    d. specific deterrence

20. Which of the following is LEAST effective in assuring deterrence?
    a. swiftness
    b. certainty
    c. proximity
    d. severity*

21. Mandatory sentencing for drug offenders is doing each of the following EXCEPT
    a. reducing drug abuse in the U.S.*
    b. crowding federal prisons.
    c. creating larger racial imbalances in prison populations.
    d. denying judges discretion in sentencing.

22. Which of the following gives the trial court judge the most power over sentencing?
    a. mandatory sentencing
    b. presumptive sentencing
    c. determinate sentencing*
    d. indeterminate sentencing

23. Presumptive sentencing:
    a. is controlled by a set of guidelines.
    b. is based on the offense and the offender's legal history.
    c. places the power to set punishment in the hands of a commission.
    d. is all of the above.*

24. When laws are passed to draw a line between respectable citizens and outcasts, the _____ justification of punishment is at work.
    a. expiation
    b. retribution
    c. restitution
    d. boundary-setting*

25. _____ repays the victim for material and financial losses suffered as a result of crime; its concern is more with the victim than the offender.
    a. Retribution
    b. Expiation
    c. Restitution*
    d. All of the above

26. A presumptive sentence is one that:
    a. allows the judge only a small amount of discretion in fixing an offender's penalty.*
    b. is based on the rehabilitation needs of the offender.
    c. assumes the offender is guilty of more crimes than those for which he was convicted.
    d. is all of the above simultaneously.

27. "Truth-in-sentencing" laws require:

    a. that only people with special training in criminal law be allowed to sit on juries.
    b. that the legal penalties for each crime be advertised by the media.
    c. that offenders serve at least 50% of their sentence before they are eligible for release.*
    d. all of the above.

28. A "concurrent" sentence:

    a. orders the inmate to serve separate sentences for his crimes in sequence.
    b. orders the inmate to serve separate sentences at the same time.*
    c. gives the judge no choice as to the length of sentence.
    d. is none of the above.

29. Three "consecutive" 5-year sentences could result in as much as _____ being served.

    a. 5 years
    b. 15 years*
    c. 30 years
    d. none of the above

30. _____ sentences used to punish certain crimes in many jurisdictions give judges virtually no discretion in assigning sentences; everyone convicted of the same crime gets exactly the same sentence under this approach.

    a. Mandatory*
    b. Presumptive
    c. Determinate
    d. Indeterminate

31. The _____ controls the penalty for crimes punished with a mandatory sentence.

    a. governor or president
    b. trial court judge
    c. legislature*
    d. prison or parole authorities

32. The _____ controls the penalty for crimes punished with an indeterminate sentence.

    a. governor or president
    b. trial court judge
    c. legislature
    d. prison or parole authorities*

33. Indeterminate sentencing is preferred by the scientific approach because:
    a. it allows sentences to be customized to the offender's unique risks and needs.
    b. it gives offenders a reason to work at their treatment and obey prison rules.
    c. it allows sentences to vary with the level of responsibility assigned to the offender.
    d. all of the above.*

34. _____ laws allow inmates to earn early release on parole through good behavior and hard work.
    a. Liberal
    b. Lenient
    c. Good time*
    d. Justice model

35. Indeterminate sentencing is associated with the _____ model of sentencing.
    a. legal
    b. scientific*
    c. liberal
    d. conservative

36. The most marked of the contradictions between philosophies of punishments is between
    a. deterrence and incapacitation.
    b. retribution and deterrence.
    c. retribution and rehabilitation.*
    d. restitution and boundary-setting.

37. For every truly dangerous person that is jailed under preventive detention laws, approximately _____ false positives are also held.
    a. two*
    b. five
    c. ten
    d. twenty-five

38. The goal of "preventive detention" is primarily:
    a. retribution.
    b. incapacitation.*
    c. expiation.
    d. restitution.

39. The most dramatic increases in the U.S. rate of imprisonment occurred in the:
    a. 1850s
    b. 1890s
    c. 1950s
    d. 1980s*

40. Islamic *Sharia* uses _____ to set the level of punishment for a specific offense.
    a. religious definitions
    b. the amount or type of proof offered
    c. both of the above*
    d. neither of the above

True-False Items

1. Punishment is the most effective way of improving a person's behavior.
   a. True
   b. False*

2. Attempts to morally equalize the wrong done by an offense by allowing, and even advertising, vengeance against the offender are justified by the concept of restitution.
   a. True
   b. False*

3. General deterrence attempts to make an example of known offenders in order to reduce the likelihood and rate of undesirable behavior in the general population.
   a. True*
   b. False

4. Changing an offender into a person who can lead a productive life in conventional society is called deterrence.
   a. True
   b. False*

5. Moral arguments for punishment focus on the search for justice and the role of the justice process in righting the wrongs done by offenders.
   a. True
   b. False*

6. The scientific model is concerned mainly with deterrence and equality in punishment.
   a. True
   b. False*

7. The logic of the legal model supports both deterrence and civil liberties.
   a. True*
   b. False

8. Indeterminate sentencing is based on the logic of the scientific model.
   a. True
   b. False*

9. Both deterrence and retribution are based on the logic of science.
   a. True
   b. False*

10. Mandatory sentencing to prison is helping to ease the crowding problems in the criminal justice system.
    a. True
    b. False*

11. Mandatory sentencing leaves no discretion to the judge.
    a. True*
    b. False

12. The federal government uses indeterminate sentencing for all crimes.
    a. True
    b. False*

13. Most federal crimes are punished with presumptive sentences.
    a. True*
    b. False

14. A presumptive sentence is one that allows the judge only a small amount of discretion in fixing an offender's penalty.
    a. True*
    b. False

15. Parole or prison authorities control the penalty for crimes punished with an indeterminate sentence.
    a. True*
    b. False

Essay and Discussion Items

1. How do politics affect the organization and policies of correctional agencies?
2. What are the major contradictions between effective behavior change and punishment?
3. What are the major assumptions of policies that stress incapacitation?
4. What are the major assumptions of policies that stress deterrence?
5. How do the media affect American correctional policy?
6. What is the "prediction problem" and how does it affect current attempts to control crime?
7. Distinguish the "scientific" approach to corrections from the "legal" one. What are the main goals and methods of each? What does each presume about the causes of crime?

Chapter Two

The History of Punishment

Learning Objectives

1. Describe the factors that made crime, law, and punishment serious concerns for human societies.
2. Explain how different justifications of punishment guided social responses to crime during the Roman Empire, Medieval era, and Enlightenment period.
3. Describe the types of punishments used in western societies prior to 1830.
4. Trace the development of the prison and link it to specific eras of United States history.
5. Discuss the role of private businesses on the development of corrections.
6. Explain why people of color have a different perspective on criminal justice than whites.
7. Link economics and popular beliefs to specific types of prisons.
8. Describe the role of the courts in shaping the modern prison.

Chapter Outline

The Origins of Punishment
    Punishment in Ancient Societies
      Corporal Punishment
    Christianity and the Medieval Era
    Medieval Law and the Growth of Crime
      English Gaols
The Age of Enlightenment
The Industrial Revolution and Modern Corrections
    Punishment and Law in Colonial America
American Prisons
    The Pennsylvania System
    The Auburn System
    The Era of the "Big House"
    The Reformatory Prison
    Corrections in the South

Major Points

1. Concern with crime and punishment appears only after humans build cities and the family's power as a social control mechanism is diminished.

2. Early legal codes relied on retribution and deterrence as their central justifications of punishment but crime continued to increase with urbanization despite dramatic increases in the frequency and severity of corporal and capital punishments.

3. Use of imprisonment, stressing isolation, penance, hard work, and discipline as treatment, began as a humane alternative to earlier methods of punishment.

4. Overcrowding led to the demise of the early expiative system and has plagued the U.S. since it first began to use imprisonment as its main response to crime.

5. Reform movements driven by fear of crime, new ideas about human behavior, humanitarian ideals, and economic problems have led to major changes in correctional practices but none has managed to significantly reduce the level of crime.

6. Abuses of human rights were routine in U.S. prisons, especially in the South, until the courts began to enforce the limited civil rights of inmates in the late 1960s.

7. As informal social control becomes less able to regulate behavior, governments take more responsibility for controlling individuals and prisons become attractive to democracies because they are the easiest way to control criminals and to keep them out of sight.

8. The dramatic increases in U.S. prison populations that began in 1980 could lead to serious economic problems in many jurisdictions.

Key Terms

Auburn system
Capital punishment
Civil service
Corporal punishment
Enlightenment
Expiation
Gaols
Good time laws
Greatest happiness principle
Hands-off era
King's Peace

Lease system
Lex talionis
Pennsylvania system
Positivism
Rate of imprisonment
Reform
Rights versus privileges
Spoils system
System expansion
Utilitarianism
Workhouses

Chapter Highlights

This chapter traces the development of crime and punishment from hunter-gatherer bands through the present day. Crime and the advent of state-controlled punishment is linked to the emergence of cities and the increasing importance of the individual as a social unit. Roman and Christian influences are reviewed along with the medieval concepts that most influenced the current structure of the justice system. The ideas of the classical school are covered in some detail as the impact of industrialization on social responses to crime is examined. The Pennsylvania and Auburn systems are presented and their decline is explained before the slavery-lease model of the South and the reformatory ideal of Elmira are introduced. The reforms of the progressive era are described and special attention is given to the treatment of women and minorities. The use of execution emerges at several points in these discussions as do comments on relevant social and economic issues that affected correctional practices. The emergence of community corrections is also given special treatment. The end of the hands-off era is covered and the courts' partial retreat from the reforms of the due process revolution are reviewed along with the basic methods of dealing with overcrowding.

Examination Questions

Multiple Choice Items

1. Knowledge of history is vital to the study of corrections because:
   a. it helps us avoid the mistakes of the past.
   b. it helps to explain why the system is organized in a particular way.
   c. it helps to predict the effects of new programs and policies.
   d. all of the above.*

2. When humans began to_____, the family began to lose its social control power, and crime became a problem.
   a. form governments
   b. live in cities*
   c. value cultural diversity
   d. devalue religion

3. In ancient civilizations, the punishments demanded by the written legal codes depended at least partly on:
   a. the emperor's mood.
   b. the offender's status.*
   c. the place in which the crime occurred.
   d. all of the above.

4. Throughout the Middle Ages the severity of punishment _____ as crime became more of a problem.
   a. decreased
   b. remained the same
   c. increased*
   d. disappeared

5. The concept of the "King's Peace":
   a. made the state the victim of all crimes.*
   b. encouraged a humanitarian approach to crime control.
   c. was based on retribution.
   d. was all of the above.

6. Public mutilation and execution had _____ effect on the crime rate while England was urbanizing.
   a. a huge
   b. no*
   c. a small
   d. a negative

7. From ancient times up until the 1800s punishments were usually:
   a. corporal.
   b. capital.
   c. financial.
   d. all of the above.*

8. Incarceration became the main form of punishment in the:
   a. Roman Empire.
   b. Biblical times.
   c. early 1800s.*
   d. early 1900s.

9. _____ is the doctrine that says all government decisions should be designed to produce the greatest pleasure for the largest number of citizens.
   a. Communism

    b. Utilitarianism*

    c. Hedonism

    d. Industrialism

10. The assumptions and logic that lead us to believe punishment can deter future crime also form the basis for:

    a. the civil liberties found in the Bill of Rights.*

    b. use of the military in crime control.

    c. treatment.

    d. all of the above.

11. Many of the principles embodied in the U.S. Constitution and Bill of Rights originated in:

    a. the classical school of thought.*

    b. the positive school of democratic thought.

    c. the Quaker religion.

    d. all of the above.

12. Indeterminate sentences were first used in the United States by:

    a. Alexander Machanochie

    b. Benjamin Rush

    c. Walter Crofton

    d. Zebulon Brockway*

13. The Classical school supported each of the following EXCEPT:

    a. deterrence

    b. civil liberties

    c. torture*

    d. utilitarianism

14. The English decision to replace capital punishment with incarceration as the main form of punishment resulted from:

    a. the observation that the executions were not deterring crime.*

    b. the belief that execution was not humane.

    c. the expense of executing offenders.

    d. public revulsion at the brutality of execution.

15. _____ in the U.S. first replaced corporal punishment with imprisonment for religious reasons.

    a. Catholics

    b. Quakers*

    c. Moslems

    d. Jews

16. The Pennsylvania system was also known as the:

    a. segregate system.*

    b. congregate system.

    c. punitive system.

    d. rehabilitative system.

17. The Auburn system was also known as the:
    a. segregate system.
    b. congregate system.*
    c. punitive system.
    d. rehabilitative system.

18. Both the Pennsylvania and Auburn systems were based on the use of:
    a. complete isolation.
    b. expiation.*
    c. corporal punishment to enforce rules.
    d. all of the above.

19. The doctrines that guided the organization and practices of early U.S. prisons:
    a. separation, discipline, and labor.*
    b. revenge, deterrence, and democracy.
    c. determinate sentences, corporal punishment, and rehabilitation.
    d. all of the above.

20. Supporters of the Auburn, or congregate, system argued that it made
    _____ for the state.
    a. justice
    b. punishment
    c. money*
    d. good publicity

21. Pennsylvania system inmates were forbidden to:
    a. work or have recreation.
    b. avoid rehabilitative counseling.
    c. communicate with others.*
    d. shave.

22. The Auburn system differed from that developed in Pennsylvania in its:
    a. profitability.
    b. use of supervised group work by inmates.
    c. use of corporal punishment to enforce rules.
    d. all of the above.*

23. Southern prisons from the civil war until the early 1900s were based on the
    _____ model of organization.
    a. military
    b. slavery*
    c. industrial
    d. reformatory

24. After the Civil War, many Southern jurisdictions:
    a. leased inmates to private businesses.
    b. used inmate labor to rebuild damage done by the war.
    c. used criminal justice to control ex-slaves.

    d. ignored the requirements of federal law.

    e. all of the above.*

25. Which of the following is NOT true of Southern lease camps:

    a. They had low rates of recidivism.*

    b. They were so filthy and oppressive that government inspectors would not enter them.

    c. They treated prisoners in grossly unjust ways.

    d. They violated federal laws.

26. Prisons of the reformatory era operated under the philosophy of:

    a. restitution.

    b. incapacitation.

    c. rehabilitation.*

    d. deterrence.

    e. expiation.

27. The "reform" approach to rehabilitation:

    a. Uses all ethical means to force an offender to change.*

    b. Allows offenders to guide their own treatment.

    c. Presumes offenders are victims of society.

    d. All of the above.

28. Meaningful and profitable prison labor was outlawed as a result of:

    a. Supreme Court rulings during the Due Process Revolution.

    b. lawsuits by business and labor unions in the late 1800s.*

    c. religious objections to profiting from misery in the early 1900s.

    d. government concerns about prison security in the last 30 years.

29. The positivists tried to use _____ to solve social problems.

    a. law

    b. religion

    c. science*

    d. all of the above

30. Positivism stressed _____ rather than deterrence.

    a. treatment

    b. prevention

    c. both of the above*

    d. neither of the above

31. The "Progressive Era" saw conditions for _____ improve in most states.

    a. women*

    b. minorities

    c. criminal suspects

    d. all of the above

32. The Great Depression led to:
    a. bans on the sale of prison-made goods.*
    b. an increase in crime larger than any experienced before or since that era.
    c. greater emphasis on crime prevention.
    d. the use of inmate labor to help build state treasuries.

33. Warehouse and Big House prisons were primarily places for _____ offenders.
    a. rehabilitating
    b. torturing
    c. incapacitating*
    d. working

34. The Federal Bureau of Prisons was created in response to _____ in state and local institutions.
    a. use of the lease system
    b. overcrowding
    c. corruption and abuses
    d. all of the above*

35. The Due Process Revolution helped professionalize corrections by making practitioners aware of the importance of:
    a. ethics.*
    b. retribution.
    c. incapacitation.
    d. vengeance.

36. The _____ doctrine maintains that rights require constitutional protection but privileges may be granted or withdrawn at the discretion of the agency.
    a. hands-off
    b. social death
    c. rights-versus-privilege*
    d. due process

37. The _____ doctrine allowed the courts to ignore prison conditions and practices for most of this nation's history by placing state prisons beyond the power of federal courts.
    a. dead to the world
    b. hands-off*
    c. Meliankoff
    d. all of the above

38. The _____ Amendment was NOT important to the prison case law that developed during the due process revolution.
    a. First
    b. Eighth

    c. Ninth*

    d. Fourteenth

39. Which of the following BEST describes the current relationship between prisons/jails and the courts?

    a. The "hands-on" era in which the courts intervene freely in correctional matters.

    b. The "hands-off" era meaning that the courts do not intervene in corrections unless there is criminal activity on the part of correctional employees.

    c. The "one hand on-one hand off" era in which the courts intervene cautiously and only when a clear threat to basic rights exists.*

    d. None of the above, we now operate under the "rights vs. privileges" doctrine.

40. Racial inequalities in prison populations rose much more dramatically between _____ than during any other period of U.S. history.

    a. 1900 and 1920

    b. 1800 and 1825

    c. 1960 and 1970

    d. 1980 and 1995*

True-False Items

1. The idea that "punishment" is the most appropriate response to rule violations is found in all societies.

    a. True

    b. False*

2. The history of crime parallels that of urbanization; as cities grow so does the crime problem.

    a. True*

    b. False

3. In ancient times, punishments depended partly on the status of the victim and the offender.

    a. True*

    b. False

4. The state became the technical "victim" of crime under the doctrine of the "King's Peace" in the Middle Ages.

    a. True*

    b. False

5. The death penalty was crucial in reducing crime as England became an urban society in the period between 1600 and 1840.

    a. True

    b. False*

6. Early Supreme Court rulings forced the U.S. to abandon corporal and capital punishment in favor of more humane sanctions like imprisonment.
   a. True
   b. False*

7. Both the Pennsylvania and Auburn systems used social isolation to achieve expiation.
   a. True*
   b. False

8. The Pennsylvania system was cheaper than the Auburn system and dominated corrections in the U.S. prior to the Civil War.
   a. True
   b. False*

9. From the Civil War until the early 1900s Southern prisons were based on the slavery-lease model even though the goal of reform predominated elsewhere.
   a. True*
   b. False

10. The "reform" approach to rehabilitation allows offenders to guide their own treatment and presumes them to be victims of social inequality.
    a. True
    b. False*

11. The status of the offenders and the victim determined the level of punishment up until the Enlightenment.
    a. True*
    b. False

12. American experiments with imprisonment as a punishment preceded the commitment to expiative systems in southern Europe under the Catholic Church.
    a. True*
    b. False

13. Early juvenile courts often forced recent immigrants to "Americanize" their children.
    a. True*
    b. False

14. Minorities won many civil rights and eliminated many forms of official oppression during the Progressive Era.
    a. True
    b. False*

15. The use of prison labor to make a profit for the state was first banned as a result of the due process revolution.
    a. True
    b. False*

Essay and Discussion Questions

1. What forces encourage a society to allow the government to use punishment to control crime?

2. What philosophies of punishment guided the development of corrections in western societies?

3. What were the main contributions of the Enlightenment to corrections?

4. What should we learn from past attempts to privatize corrections and make prisons profitable?

5. How have economics affected the development of prisons in the U.S.?

6. How did the due process revolution affect prisons?

7. What forces are causing racial imbalances in modern prison populations?

8. Explain why U.S. prison populations have grown so dramatically since 1980 and list three common methods of responding to overcrowding.

Chapter Three

Jails

Learning Objectives

1. Distinguish between jails and other types of long- and short-term correctional facilities.
2. Describe the basic design features of a jail.
3. Explain why local control of jails leads to problems in funding, staffing, and administration.
4. List the possible legal statuses of jail inmates.
5. Describe three ways by which a person might be released from jail prior to trial.
6. Explain why so many jail inmates are mentally ill.
7. Discuss the problem of jail suicide from legal and behavioral perspectives.
8. Discuss the main methods used in the U.S. today to reduce jail costs.

Chapter Outline

The Development of Jails
Modern Jails
    Physical Design and Organization
    Local Administration
    Inmates' Legal Statuses
    Jail Programs
Methods of Pre-trial Release
    Bail
    Release on Recognizance
    Pre-trial Supervision
    Alternatives to Jail
The Inmate Experience
    The Mentally Ill in Jail
        Criminalization and Medicalization Theses
Jail Suicides

Major Points

1. Jails are the oldest type of penal confinement facility and usually hold social outcasts as well as serious offenders.

2. All jails have a sallyport, holding tank, and book-in area. Some segregate staff from inmates but the more modern "new-generation" jail places detention officers in the podular unit with the inmates to prevent problems.

3. Inmates may be awaiting trial, sentencing, or transport to a prison, or they may be serving a sentence for a misdemeanor.

4. Jails are usually operated by county law enforcement agencies that have little interest in corrections. Staff are also likely to be oriented more to policing than corrections.

5. Persons awaiting trail may be released by posting bail, obtaining release on recognizance from a magistrate, or by participating in a pre-trial release and supervision program.

6. The experience of being jailed is disorienting and disorganizing for inmates, many of whom are already suffering from mental illness. The use of jails to control the mentally ill is also of concern.

7. Detention officers are the least well-paid and trained people in the criminal justice system despite the fact that jails are used by more justice agencies than any other type of facility.

8. Many jurisdictions are trying to reduce jail costs by privatizing all or part of their jail's operations and/or charging inmates for services and room and board. Inter-jurisdictional space leasing arrangements are also of growing import in addressing jail crowding.

Key Terms

Administrative segregation

Bail

Clear and convincing evidence

Conditional release programs

Criminalization thesis

Day fines

Diversion

Holding facilities

Intermittent sentences

Medicalization thesis

New-generation jail

Pre-trial detainees

Punitive segregation

Release on recognizance

Sallyport

Stockade

Trustee

Work release

Chapter Highlights

Jails are distinguished from other types of penal facilities and the unique aspects of their development are reviewed. The basic physical components of a jail are described and the new-generation jail is introduced. The problems posed by the local administration of jails by law enforcement authorities is discussed before the legal statuses and demographic traits of jail inmates are covered. Methods of release from jail prior to trial, such as bail, release on recognizance, and pre-trial supervision, are outlined and some alternatives to jail are briefly discussed. The effects of the jail environment on inmates is described and the growing impact of the mentally ill on jail populations is explained. The dangers of jail suicide are given some attention as is the role of the detention officer and the legal regulation of jails. Attention finally turns to current methods of cutting jail costs such as privatization, fee-for-service programs, and interjurisdictional space leasing arrangements.

Examination Questions

Multiple Choice Items

1. _____ are institutions in which suspects can be detained for up to forty-eight hours before being released or transferred to a facility that can provide long-term custody.
   a. Prisons
   b. Holding facilities*
   c. Jails
   d. Asylums

2. The entrance used by police officers bringing prisoners to the facility is called:
   a. a breezeway.
   b. a sallyport.*
   c. an entry ramp.
   d. a bull pen.

3. The term _____ refers to a large holding cell near the central book-in area that is used to confine newly-arrived prisoners.
   a. breezeway
   b. sallyport
   c. entry ramp
   d. bull pen*

4. For their own safety, _____ persons can be neither released nor placed in the main area of the jail.
   a. mentally ill
   b. drug addicted
   c. intoxicated*
   d. homeless

5. _____ are inmates who are considered to be low risks to security and get special privileges in exchange for working around the jail or on projects in the community.
   a. Felons
   b. Trustees*
   c. Misdemeanants
   d. Squirrels

6. A stockade is:
   a. a minimum security jail from which work programs are operated.*
   b. a police outpost in a high crime area.
   c. a prison for long-term inmates.
   d. a military jail or prison.

7. Jails usually compete with roads and schools for funding because they are:
   a. funded primarily at the local level.*
   b. funded primarily at the state level.
   c. require little financial aid.
   d. are well-staffed with many programs for inmates.

8. Conditions in jails for the unconvicted are often _____ those in prisons housing convicted felons.
   a. better than
   b. worse than*
   c. the same as

9. Most American jails are funded and administered by _____ agencies.
   a. city
   b. county*
   c. state
   d. federal

10. Which of the following might be found incarcerated in a jail?
    a. accused persons awaiting trial.
    b. convicted persons awaiting sentencing.
    c. convicted misdemeanants serving their sentence.
    d. sentenced felons awaiting transport to state prison.
    e. any and all of the above.*

11. The majority of people held in jails are:
    a. pre-trial detainees.*
    b. convicted felons.
    c. convicted misdemeanants.
    d. material witnesses.

12. At least _____ percent of those in U.S. jails are incarcerated as a result of the war on drugs.
    a. 10
    b. 30*
    c. 60
    d. 90

13. Which of the following is LESS common in a jail than a prison?
    a. mentally ill inmates.
    b. serious offenders.*
    c. female offenders.
    d. marginal criminals.

14. Jails are most likely to offer:
    a. drug treatment programs.
    b. services for the mentally ill.
    c. basic life skills like literacy.*
    d. all of the above.

15. Which of the following offenses have contributed the LEAST to jail crowding?
    a. drug crimes.
    b. drunken driving.
    c. nuisance crimes like vagrancy.
    d. predatory crimes like burglary.*

16. Pre-trial detainees can be released before their court date through the use of:
    a. bail.
    b. pre-trial release programs.
    c. personal recognizance.
    d. any of the above.*

17. _____ is a financial guarantee that a person will return for trial that is available to most suspects in all jurisdictions.
    a. Bail*
    b. Pre-trial release programs
    c. Personal recognizance
    d. Any of the above

18. Pre-trial release programs are usually administered by:
    a. the police or sheriff's department.
    b. the probation department.*
    c. a private company.
    d. the welfare department.

19. _____ allows a magistrate to free a suspect on his or her promise to return for court dates.
    a. Bail
    b. Pre-trial release programs
    c. Release on recognizance*
    d. any of the above.

20. _____ sentences allow convicted offenders to work during the day and spend nights and/or weekends in jail.
    a. Probation
    b. Intermittent*
    c. Stockade
    d. Restitution

21. Which of the following is a problem encountered by jail inmates?
    a. disintegration
    b. disorientation
    c. degradation
    d. preparation for underclass life
    e. all of the above*

22. The **criminalization thesis** holds that:
    a. jails have replaced mental hospitals as places for confining the mentally ill.*
    b. society defines too many acts as criminal.
    c. a larger percentage of each succeeding generation is criminal.
    d. jails and prisons increase a person's criminality.

23. Mentally ill people who commit _____ crimes are locked away by police because there is no other convenient way of handling them.
    a. felonious
    b. heinous
    c. marginal*
    d. misdemeanor

24. It is estimated that _____ is 5 to 10 times more common among jail inmates than in the general population due to the terrible physical conditions and embarrassment of being arrested and booked.
    a. drug use
    b. suicide*
    c. alcoholism
    d. murder

25. _____ is the most common cause of death among jail inmates.
    a. Suicide
    b. Homicide
    c. AIDS
    d. Natural causes*

26. Which of the following is a predictor of suicide among jail inmates?
    a. a history of previous suicide attempts.
    b. symptoms of depression.
    c. intoxication, especially when due to alcohol.
    d. situations in which incarceration presents a life-shattering crisis to the person.
    e. any of the above.*

27. The legal regulation of jails is:
    a. very strict in most states.
    b. performed by the courts.
    c. minimal.*
    d. maximal.

28. A detention officer's normal routine includes:
    a. a variety of paperwork.
    b. conducting rounds to assure all is well in the cell blocks.
    c. searching cells for drugs and weapons.
    d. escorting inmates to treatment programs or other appointments.
    e. all of the above.*

29. Jail guards are usually described as _____ officers.
    a. corrections
    b. detention*
    c. police
    d. sheriffs

30. Detention officers are the _____ educated, trained, and paid group of correctional employees.
    a. least*
    b. best

31. _____ has long been the main method for assuring that a small number of officers can keep a large number of inmates under constant control over a long period of time.
    a. Architecture*
    b. Mortification
    c. Use of force
    d. Religion

32. _____ keeps contact between detention officers and inmates at the lowest possible level in most facilities.
    a. Crowding

b. Architectural design*

c. Inmate and employee turnover

d. All of the above

33. _____ are self-contained living areas made up of individual cells and an open area for socializing and/or recreation.

a. Cell blocks

b. Podular units*

c. Super segregation units

d. Stockades

34. The mark of a *new-generation jail* lies in:

a. the attitudes and training of the employees.

b. the design used to promote direct interaction between guards and inmates.

c. both of the above.*

d. neither of the above.

35. Popular alternatives to jail consist of:

a. fines and restitution or community service.

b. detoxification centers.

c. work release and/or intermittent sentences.

d. diversion programs.

e. all of the above.*

36. Day fines allow judges to set the amount of an offender's fine on the basis of:

a. the seriousness of the offense.

b. the offender's ability to pay the fine.

c. both of the above.*

d. neither of the above.

37. Popular methods of reducing jail costs currently include:

a. privatization.

b. leasing space from other jurisdictions.

c. charging inmates for services.

d. all of the above.*

38. Which of the following is LEAST effective in reducing jail costs?

a. replacing staff with technology.*

b. adopting "new generation" design and training.

c. privatizing some services.

d. using trustee labor.

39. Which of the following is NOT true of the practice of charging inmates for room, board, and services?

a. It places a financial burden on some of the poorest people in our society.

b. It is popular because it is tough on suspected offenders.

c. It has been declared unconstitutional by the federal courts.*

d. It may lead to recidivism as well as burden their families and the welfare system.

40. When jails hold prisoners from other states:
    a. prisonization is increased by lack of visitors.
    b. boredom becomes a serious problem.
    c. security may not be adequate.
    d. all of the above.*

True-False Items

1. A jail may hold suspects for only forty-eight hours.
   a. True
   b. False*

2. The entrance used by police officers bringing prisoners to the facility is called a sallyport.
   a. True*
   b. False

3. Control of jail inmates is difficult because so many are sick, injured, or intoxicated.
   a. True
   b. False*

4. Only people who are sober and reasonably healthy may be placed in the general population of a jail.
   a. True*
   b. False

5. Trustees are inmates who are considered to be low risks to security and get special privileges in exchange for working around the jail or on projects in the community.
   a. True*
   b. False

6. Jails rarely have trouble with funding because they are locally controlled.
   a. True
   b. False*

7. Most jails have comprehensive programs for the mentally ill and chemically dependent.
   a. True
   b. False*

8. The majority of people held in jails are pre-trial detainees.
   a. True*
   b.False

9. Most of the people held in jails are charged with drug offenses.
   a. True
   b. False*

10. Jail inmates are more often charged with "nuisance" crimes than with serious felonies.
    a. True*
    b. False
11. Release on recognizance allows a magistrate to free a suspect on his or her promise to return for court dates.
    a. True*
    b. False
12. The medicalization thesis holds that jails have replaced mental hospitals as places for confining the mentally ill.
    a. True
    b. False*
13. The criminalization thesis holds that jails have replaced mental hospitals as places for confining the mentally ill.
    a. True*
    b. False
14. Suicide is far more common among jail inmates than among those in prisons.
    a. True*
    b. False
15. The use of private companies to handle part of a jail's operation, such as food services or medical care, is a very new development in U.S. corrections.
    a. True
    b. False*

Essay and Discussion Items

1. Trace the development of jails from ancient to modern times. What problems led to major changes in the operation of these facilities?
2. Into what legal status groups can jail inmates be divided?
3. What are the main problems in the routine operation of a jail? How are these related to local control by law enforcement agencies?
4. What is bail? What other methods are used to assure appearance at trial for defendants released from jail?
5. What is life like for jail inmates? What are inmates most likely to learn while in jail?
6. Why are so many jail inmates classified as mentally ill? What problems do these inmates pose for jailers?
7. What distinguishes a "new-generation" jail from other types of jails?
8. What methods could we use to reduce the use of jails for minor offenders?
9. By what methods might a county try to reduce jail costs?

Chapter Four

Probation

Learning Objectives

1. List the main goals of probation.
2. Describe the traits of probationers and compare them with those of prisoners.
3. List the criteria used to select offenders for probation. Describe the legal factors that often affect this selection.
4. Explain the various ways in which a probation sentence may be imposed.
5. Discuss the training as well as the investigative, rehabilitative, and supervisory duties of a probation officer.
6. Explain the difference between criminal and technical violations of probation and distinguish between standard and special conditions.
7. Describe the legal rights of probationers and the procedures used in revoking probation.
8. Discuss the various types of probation caseloads and the frequency of revocation in each.

Chapter Outline

Goals of Probation
    Traits and Offenses of Probationers
Probation and Ideology
Methods of Imposing Probation
    The Conditions of Probation
    Violations of Probation
Revocation of Probation
The Probation Process
    Probation Investigations
    Probation Supervision
      Office Visits
      Field Visits
      Treatment Coordination

Major Points

1. Probation is less injurious than prison and far cheaper if the offender is unlikely to commit serious crimes.

2. Probation is a contract that a court may offer to a defendant in lieu of imprisonment; the conditions of probation are the terms of that contract and their violation can lead to revocation.

3. Revocation of probation is much easier to obtain than a criminal conviction and probationers enjoy fewer due process rights than criminal defendants.

4. Probation officers investigate defendants, make sentencing recommendations to judges, supervise offenders released to the community, and coordinate their treatment.

5. The trial court has almost complete authority over the selection of probationers and the terms of probation but most probation officers work for the state department of correction. A few states allow trial courts to directly control probation, however.

6. The normal adult probation officer has a caseload of around 100 clients but caseloads vary widely with the level or type of supervision required by the court.

7. Probation officers are evaluated on how well they keep the records on each offender-client and must attend annual training events to keep their skills and knowledge up to date.

Key Terms

Absconder
Community corrections
Conditions of probation
Caseload
Deferred adjudication
Field visits
In-service training

Presentence investigation
Revocation of probation
Shock probation
Special conditions
Split sentence
Standard conditions
Technical violation

Chapter Summary

Probation allows offenders to build and maintain ties to the law-abiding community while receiving treatment and being supervised by a correctional professional. Some see it as an inexpensive way to give offenders a second chance before experiencing imprisonment. The trial court imposes a set of conditions on the offender as a condition of release. A probation officer then works with the offender to assure that these conditions are met. New crimes or violations of the conditions can lead to stricter supervision or loss of freedom. Revocation of probation requires only a majority of evidence suggesting guilt and has fewer procedural protections than a trial. Probation officers also investigate defendants prior to sentencing and provide judges with recommendations on sentencing and terms of supervision. Supervision consists of home and field visits, the frequency of which are determined by the level of supervision set by the court. The PO also coordinates the offender's treatment. The probation department is usually part of the state's department of correction but may also be controlled by local courts. Probation officers must keep thorough records, manage the activities of the offenders; annual in-service training allows them to keep pace with changes in their responsibilities.

Examination Questions

Multiple Choice Items

1. Community corrections is made up of _____ agencies.
   a. prison and police
   b. parole and probation*
   c. jail and prison
   d. all of the above

2. _____ is the most common sentence for non-traffic offenses in the U.S.
   a. Jail
   b. Prison
   c. Probation*
   d. Parole

3. Which of the following is a major goal of probation?
   a. reduce correctional costs.
   b. provide restitution.
   c. reduce the damage done by imprisonment.
   d. encourage rehabilitation and reintegration.
   e. all of the above.*

4. Probation supervision is usually controlled by:
   a. the state department of correction.*
   b. the sentencing court.

    c. treatment providers.

    d. all of the above jointly.

5. Probationers are more often _____ than are prison or jail inmates.

    a. older and poorer

    b. black or Hispanic

    c. white and female*

    d. all of the above

6. In response to conservative criticism of its treatment orientation, probation is becoming _____ in many jurisdictions.

    a. less frequent

    b. more punishment oriented*

    c. more religiously focused

    d. all of the above

7. Which of the following may affect the decision as to whether an offender receives probation?

    a. the availability of specific programs and services in the local area.

    b. the philosophy of the sentencing court.

    c. the availability of prison or jail cells.

    d. all of the above.*

8. Probation may be given as a result of plea bargaining when:

    a. the prosecutor's case is weak.

    b. the victim is unwilling to testify.

    c. restitution is the main goal of sentencing.

    d. all of the above.*

9. Legally, probation conditions are a _____ offered to the offender by the court.

    a. special deal

    b. punishment

    c. contract*

    d. all of the above

10. Probation may be imposed only by:

    a. a judge.*

    b. the legislature.

    c. the governor.

    d. the police.

11. Failure to follow the conditions of parole/probation that does not actually violate the law is referred to as a _____ violation of probation/parole.

    a. misdemeanor

    b. felony

    c. technical*

    d. abscond

12. Conditions of probation are set by:
    a. the trial court judge.*
    b. the probation officer.
    c. the therapeutic triad.
    d. a special jury.

13. _____ conditions of probation are those imposed on all offenders sentenced to probation in a particular jurisdiction.
    a. Standard*
    b. Special
    c. Normal
    d. Extraordinary

14. _____ conditions of probation are those added to meet the unique concerns of controlling and rehabilitating a particular offender.
    a. Standard
    b. Special*
    c. Normal
    d. Extraordinary

15. Drug testing and/or treatment, community service, counseling, living in a residential facility, avoiding contact with the victim, or having to live under house arrest are almost always _____ conditions of probation.
    a. standard
    b. special*
    c. normal
    d. extraordinary

16. People on probation for a _____ are much more likely to complete their sentence successfully than are those on probation for:
    a. violent crime/public order crime
    b. misdemeanor/felony*
    c. felony/misdemeanor
    d. public order crime/violent crime

17. Persons who have intentionally fled or hidden themselves so that their probation officer cannot supervise them are known as:
    a. runners.
    b. technical violators.
    c. absconders.*
    d. recidivists.

18. Probationers are _____ likely to commit a new crime while under community supervision than parolees.
    a. much less*
    b. slightly less
    c. much more
    d. slightly more

19. Which of the following rights are NOT possessed by a probationer facing revocation?

    a. written notice of the charges, proceedings, and evidence to be used
    b. power to subpoena
    c. trial by jury*
    d. the right to confront accusers

20. Revocation proceedings use the _____ standard of proof to determine guilt.
    a. criminal (beyond a reasonable doubt)
    b. mental health (clear and convincing evidence)
    c. civil (majority of evidence)*
    d. none of the above

21. Which of the following was most critical in defining the rights of a probationer facing revocation?

    a. *Ruiz v. Estelle*
    b. *Mapp v. Ohio*
    c. *Gagnon v. Scarpelli**
    d. *Pugh v. Locke*

22. Which of the following is NOT true of revocation of probation/parole:

    a. violating any criminal law can result in revocation.
    b. violating the conditions of release can result in revocation.
    c. the majority of available evidence must indicate guilt.
    d. the offender has all the rights of a felony defendant facing trial.*

23. Which of the following is a vital part of the probation process?

    a. investigation
    b. supervision
    c. treatment coordination
    d. all of the above*

24. The role of probation/parole officer includes each of the following EXCEPT:

    a. investigating the background/living arrangements of potential releasees.
    b. monitoring the offenders' activities to assure that they are living within the law.
    c. enforcing legally mandated conditions of liberty.
    d. providing in-depth counseling to help the offender avoid future crime.*
    e. scrutinizing community programs that might meet the needs of various offenders.

25. Which of the following criteria are used to decide which offenders will receive probation?

    a. public safety
    b. treatment needs
    c. likelihood of success
    d. all of the above*

26. The Presentence Investigation Report is primarily intended to:
    a. aid judges in making sentencing decisions.*
    b. aid in reducing prison crowding by encouraging the use of probation.
    c. help the offender avoid punishment.
    d. all of the above.

27. A _____ examines the offender's background and current situation in order to estimate his/her treatment needs and the amount of danger he/she may pose to the community.
    a. presentence investigation*
    b. police investigation
    c. prosecutor's screening
    d. classification analysis

28. Office visits serve mainly to allow the officer to:
    a. collect paperwork, fees, and urine samples from the probationer.
    b. provide a safe situation in which to confront the probationer about problem behavior.
    c. both of the above.*
    d. neither of the above.

29. Field visits provide officers with the opportunity to:
    a. see how the offender lives.
    b. speak with the family and neighbors of the probationer.
    c. interact with the probationer in a relaxed setting.
    d. all of the above.*

30. Most probation service is organized at which level of government?
    a. city
    b. county
    c. state*
    d. regional

31. Federal probation officers supervise:
    a. persons released from federal prisons.
    b. persons sentenced to probation by federal courts.
    c. both of the above.*
    d. neither of the above.

32. Probation officers are usually evaluated on the basis of their:
    a. counseling skills.
    b. caseload recidivism rate.
    c. files and paperwork.*
    d. all of the above.

33. Regular _____ allow probation officers to broaden their skills and keep up with changes in the field.
    a. teaching memos
    b. in-service training sessions*

    c. attendance at college courses

    d. home study

34. The group of offenders supervised by a single probation officer is known as his/her:

    a. offender block.

    b. caseload.*

    c. duty list.

    d. millstone.

35. Which of the following best describes the average adult probation caseload in the U.S. today?

    a. about 50 clients

    b. about 100 clients*

    c. about 250 clients

    d. 400 to 500 clients

36. Small caseloads usually lead to _____ rates of revocation.

    a. increased*

    b. decreased

    c. no change in

    d. an unpredictable effect on

37. Small probation caseloads are desirable because they:

    a. help assure closer control of the offender.*

    b. are less expensive than normal probation caseloads.

    c. usually result in less recidivism.

    d. encourage POs to do more counseling.

38. Small caseloads and intensive probation supervision can result in relatively high rates of revocation for each of the following reasons EXCEPT:

    a. offenders are under closer scrutiny.

    b. high risk probationers are usually assigned to such programs.

    c. probation officers become bored and frustrated.*

    d. all of the above.

39. Probation officers with _____ supervision caseloads usually have between 20 and 40 clients.

    a. minimum

    b. administrative

    c. intensive*

    d. normal

40. To be effective, a probation officer should have a thorough knowledge of:

    a. law.

    b. offender behavior.

    c. government organization.

    d. treatment.

    e. all of the above.*

True-False Items

1. The widespread use of community-based corrections is based on both human-
    itarian and utilitarian factors.
    a. True*
    b. False

2. Even though probation caseloads are growing faster than prison populations,
    probation gets less than 10% of U.S. correctional funding.
    a. True*
    b. False

3. As a group, probationers are very similar to prison and jail inmates; they are
    predominantly minorities who have committed a felony.
    a. True
    b. False*

4. Probation becomes more oriented to treatment with every passing year.
    a. True
    b. False*

5. Probation may result from plea bargaining if the prosecutor fears losing the
    case at trial.
    a. True*
    b. False

6. Probation is a privilege that can be granted only by the governor or a special
    board.
    a. True
    b. False*

7. Revocation of probation requires only that the majority of evidence support
    the allegation that a violation occurred.
    a. True*
    b. False

8. Probationers facing revocation have all the rights of a defendant facing trial.
    a. True
    b. False*

9. Probation has always served the rehabilitative goals of corrections rather
    than the retributive or incapacitative ones.
    a. True
    b. False*

10. Probation officers spend most of their time counseling their clients and pro-
    viding other forms of support and treatment.
    a. True
    b. False*

11. Probation officers conduct investigations, supervise clients, maintain detailed records, and coordinate treatment services.
    a. True
    b. False*

12. The average adult probation officer supervises 90 to 100 clients each month.
    a. True*
    b. False

13. Presentence investigations focus mainly on the treatment needs of the offender.
    a. True
    b. False*

14. Most probation officers are employed by the state department of corrections.
    a. True*
    b. False

15. The fact that the rate of revocation usually rises when the size of caseloads is reduced indicates that small caseloads lead to poor supervision and control.
    a. True
    b. False*

Essay and Discussion Items

1. How do the theoretical goals of probation differ from the way this sanction is actually used in the U.S. today?

2. In what ways might a probation sentence be imposed? Who has authority over the probationer?

3. By what methods does a probation officer attempt to control clients' behavior?

4. What are conditions of probation? What should they be designed to accomplish?

5. Describe the process by which probation may be revoked. How does this process differ from a criminal trial? How is it similar?

6. What is the role of the probation officer in getting treatment for her/his clients?

7. What are the basic duties of a probation officer? What sort of training best prepares someone to take this role?

8. What types of caseloads might a probation officer supervise? What expectations would you have for each type? Why?

Chapter Five

Intermediate Sanctions

Learning Objectives

1. Describe the forces that led to the development of intermediate sanctions and the kind(s) of offenders for whom they are designed.
2. Describe the intermediate sanctions most common in the U.S. today and identify the specific goals that each is designed to achieve.
3. Discuss the effectiveness of each intermediate sanction in punishing, controlling, and reintegrating offenders.
4. Describe the dangers posed by intermediate sanctions.
5. Discuss the factors that predict the popularity of the various intermediate sanctions.

Chapter Outline

The Logic of Intermediate Sanctions
Selection of Clients
Types of Intermediate Sanctions
    Restitution and Community Service
    Intensive Probation/Parole Supervision Programs (ISPs)
      Specialized Caseloads
    Home Confinement and Electronic Monitoring
    Day Centers
    Split Sentences
    Correctional Boot Camps
    Therapeutic Communities
The Effectiveness of Intermediate Sanctions
The Dangers of Intermediate Sanctions
    The Growing "Culture of Surveillance"
    Opportunity Costs
    Expanding the Net of Social Control
    Discrimination in the Use of Intermediate Sanctions
    Counseling Versus Control
    Risk Management

Third Party Impacts
Summary

Major Points

1. Intermediate sanctions are more severe than traditional probation but less restrictive than incarceration; they are designed to cut prison costs while avoiding prisonization.

2. Each intermediate sanction has specific goals: intensive supervision and day reporting centers are for incapacitation, boot camps should incapacitate and deter, restitution and community service compensate victims or society, and therapeutic communities offer intense treatment.

3. Intermediate sanctions are often used to make probation more punishing rather than to reduce prison populations, which makes them less cost-effective than originally hoped.

4. Dangers of intermediate sanctions include expanding the net of social control and technological surveillance, assuring failure of persons under community supervision, unrecognized opportunity costs and increasing the stress of punishment at the cost of effective treatment. Some sentences also affect third parties who have committed no crime.

Key Terms

Back door programs	Home confinement
Boot camp	Home detention
Community service	Intensive supervision
Culture of surveillance	Net of social control
Day reporting centers	Opportunity costs
Electronic monitoring	Restitution
Front-door programs	Shock probation
Graduated sanctions	Specialized caseloads
Halfway houses	Therapeutic community

Chapter Summary

Many states use a graduated series of punishments that provide levels of control and punishment that are more stringent than traditional probation but less severe than incarceration. These intermediate sanctions resulted from economic pressures and fears that imprisonment actually produces more hardened offenders. Restitution is the most common intermediate sanction in the U.S. and community service is increasingly common as well. Intensive supervision and electronically monitored home confinement are increasing in popularity. Split sentences expose the offender to incarceration briefly for deterrence purposes. Boot camps are becoming popular as part of split sentences but despite their popular appeal, their effectiveness is widely questioned. Day reporting centers have punitive and incapacitative value but are rare due to the "not in my neighborhood" reaction of citizens. Therapeutic communities are the only intermediate sanction that is primarily oriented to treatment but these residential centers are expensive and have a high drop-out rate. Intermediate sanctions are only effective in cutting costs when they are used instead of imprisonment. While they allow courts to customize probation conditions to the treatment needs of the particular offender, most are used simply to increase the punitive value of community supervision. Dangers of these sanctions include the expanding net of social control and culture of surveillance made possible by technology. We must also be wary of the potential for economic discrimination that inheres in these sanctions and remain sensitive to their opportunity costs.

Examination Questions

Multiple Choice Items

1. _____ are alternatives to prison or jail that are run by probation and parole agencies.
   a. Diversion programs
   b. Intermediate sanctions*
   c. Therapy centers
   d. All of the above

2. Implementation of programs such as intensively supervised probation, house arrest, electronic monitoring, restitution, and community service most often require:
   a. the creation of new bureaucratic agencies.
   b. more funding than imprisonment.
   c. creativity on the part of judges and probation officers.*
   d. none of the above.

3. In order to assure public safety and satisfy the demands of judges, legislators, and voters, intermediate sanctioning programs have tended to stress:
   a. counseling for psychological rehabilitation.
   b. an emphasis on employment and self-help groups for the offender.
   c. the deterrent and incapacitating characteristics of the programs.*
   d. none of the above.

4. The goals of intermediate sanctions vary according to:
   a. the goals of the agency that administers it.
   b. the beliefs of the judge or parole board that imposes it.
   c. the needs and risks posed by the particular offender to whom it is assigned.
   d. all of the above.*

5. Which of the following is not a goal of one or more intermediate sanctions?
   a. increase the probability of full rehabilitation.*
   b. provide maximum control with minimum cost.
   c. force offenders to be as accountable and responsible as possible.
   d. all of the above are common goals of intermediate sanctions.

6. Conservatives dislike high rates of imprisonment because they feel:
   a. effects of prisonization cause further crime.
   b. its financial cost is too high.*
   c. community-based services are more efficient.
   d. all of the above.

7. Liberals prefer community-based supervision/control because they feel:
   a. effects of prisonization cause further crime.
   b. its financial cost is too high.
   c. community-based services are more efficient.
   d. all of the above.*

8. A program that employs alternative sentencing prior to imprisonment is called:
   a. standard probation.
   b. a back-door approach.
   c. a front-door approach.*
   d. standard parole.

9. The _____ costs of imprisonment include welfare payments for the inmate's family and tax revenues that could have been collected if the offender had remained in the community.
   a. direct
   b. indirect*
   c. theoretical
   d. practical

10. Which of the following is a reason for the use of intermediate sanctions:
    a. Restitution can be provided more easily when offenders are held accountable for their crimes in their home community.
    b. By allowing offenders to remain free and making them work, their sense of responsibility may be increased rather than reduced as it would be in the environment of a jail or prison.
    c. Being punished in one's home community may be more effective because the family and community are more involved.
    d. Punishing offenders in the community makes more treatment and educational resources available while reducing costs.
    e. all of the above.*

11. Intermediate sanctions were created to allow:
    a. offenders to avoid the negative influences of prison.
    b. lowered correctional costs.

    c. community control to become more incapacitating.

    d. all of the above.*

12. To be cost-effective, intermediate sanctions should be used with:

    a. nonviolent offenders.

    b. persons with few prior arrests.

    c. people who have no history of imprisonment.

    d. all of the above.*

13. Which of the following limits the breadth and range of intermediate sanctions?

    a. The limits placed on corrections by the courts.

    b. The creativity of the authorities that impose them.*

    c. The fact that they are more expensive than imprisonment.

    d. The costs of creating a new agency to administer them.

14. Some agencies use the term _____ to describe a series of programs or conditions of liberty that gradually increase the punishment and intrusiveness of community corrections according to the offender's behavior.

    a. graduated sanctions*

    b. incarcerative modicums

    c. prison substitutes

    d. monitored living arrangements

15. The most popular intermediate sanction in the U.S. today is:

    a. the therapeutic community.

    b. electronic monitoring.

    c. restitution.*

    d. all of the above are equally popular.

16. Most studies indicate that restitution has _____ effect on offender recidivism rates.

    a. a large and positive

    b. no*

    c. a small but negative

    d. no studies have examined this issue.

17. Direct restitution is oriented primarily to:

    a. assisting the victim.

    b. reforming the offender.

    c. rebuilding the community.

    d. all of the above.*

19. Community service is oriented primarily to:

    a. reforming the offender.

    b. assisting the victim.

    c. (re)building the community.*

    d. all of the above.

20. Restitution payments may be distributed by any of the following EXCEPT:
    a. the state Attorney General.
    b. the probation department.
    c. the prosecutor's office.
    d. the offender.*

21. Fears of a "perpetual incarceration machine" developing within community corrections are focused on the use of:
    a. punishment rather than treatment.
    b. excessive levels of supervision.
    c. fines, fees, and restitution payments that add up to most of an offender's income.*
    d. Use of split sentences and boot camps.

22. Offenders in intensive supervision caseloads get at least _____ the attention from the probation or parole officer that normal clients receive.
    a. twice*
    b. five times
    c. ten times
    d. one hundred times

23. Offenders are usually placed on ISP because:
    a. their crimes were more serious than those of other probationers or parolees.
    b. they performed poorly under regular supervision.
    c. both of the above.*
    d. neither of the above.

24. Which of the following is NOT a reason that ISP caseloads have higher revocation rates than others?
    a. they include the poorest risks for community supervision.
    b. these offenders are watched more closely than others.
    c. they are supervised by the least skilled officers.*
    d. officers are quicker to initiate revocation proceedings against them.

25. Specialized caseloads usually consist of:
    a. sex offenders.
    b. substance abusers.
    c. mentally impaired offenders.
    d. any of the above.*

26. Specialized caseloads usually receive _____ supervision.
    a. lenient
    b. intensive*
    c. supercilious
    d. fictive

27. The best way to improve ISPs' ability to cut recidivism and prison costs would be to increase the emphasis on:
    a. punishment rather than treatment.
    b. control rather than punishment.
    c. self-esteem and personal values.
    d. drug treatment.*

28. Studies show that boot camps which stress discipline and labor rather than counseling:
    a. reduce recidivism more than probation or prison.
    b. are no more effective than probation or prison in reducing recidivism.*
    c. may actually encourage recidivism.
    d. do not exist in the U.S.

29. Day centers function to:
    a. keep unemployed offenders off the street.
    b. provide a convenient central location for service providers.
    c. assure that there will be few rewards from avoiding employment.
    d. all of the above.*

30. There are relatively few day centers in the U.S. because:
    a. the public opposes treatment.
    b. the Supreme Court says it is illegal to punish the unemployed.
    c. people do not want them near their neighborhoods.*
    d. none of the above; day centers are very common throughout the U.S.

31. Why are institutional administrators intimidated by movements toward deinstitutionalization?
    a. They fear losing an essential element of the facility's work force.
    b. They fear loss of funding through per capita formulas used by legislatures.
    c. They put the needs of their facility first.
    d. All of the above.*

32. Which of the following is the LEAST important goal of modern ISP programs?
    a. deterrence
    b. incapacitation/control
    c. retribution
    d. expiation*

33. The effectiveness of intermediate sanctions vary with:
    a. the quality of each program's staff
    b. the way in which they are imposed.
    c. the methods used to select clients.
    d. all of the above.*

34. Of all the intermediate sanctions reviewed in the text, only _____ has been shown to reduce recidivism.
    a. boot camps

b. the therapeutic community*

c. restitution

d. day reporting centers

35. Therapeutic communities differ from other alternative sentences because they:

a. are more concerned with rehabilitation than control.*

b. require the offender to live at a particular facility.

c. tolerate illegal and deviant behavior so long as no one is endangered.

d. are all of the above.

36. EMHC seems to have _____ effect on the mental health of offenders and to impact their family environment in a _____ way.

a. a slightly negative/very negative

b. no/slightly positive*

c. no/slightly negative

d. a very positive/slightly positive

37. Small probation caseloads are desirable because:

a. they encourage and facilitate high quality contacts between P.O. and offender.

b. they are less expensive to administer than normal probation caseloads.

c. they always result in less recidivism.

d. all of the above.*

38. Concern with the ethics of alternative sentencing include fears that:

a. such programs will "widen the net of social control."

b. lack sufficient value as a deterrent to crime.

c. de-emphasize rehabilitation in favor of supervision.

d. will discriminate in favor of wealthy offenders.

e. all of the above.*

39. The greatest fear of alternative sanctions is that they will _____ by encouraging the supervision of people whose crimes are so minor that they would not otherwise be placed under correctional control.

a. discriminate against the poor

b. expand the net of social control*

c. create a culture of surveillance

d. reduce the use of treatment

40. The idea of _____ requires that the benefits of a program should be compared with those of others that were not being used because of limited resources.

a. opportunity costs*

b. community service

c. net widening

d. third party impact reduction

True-False Items

1. Implementation of programs such as intensively supervised probation, house arrest, electronic monitoring, restitution, and community service most often require the creation of new bureaucratic agencies.
   a. True
   b. False*

2. Intermediate sanctions allow offenders to avoid the negative influences of the prison subculture.
   a. True*
   b. False

3. As with probation and parole in general, many criticisms of intermediate sentencing arise from poor selection procedures more than the nature of the programs.
   a. True*
   b. False

4. Alternative sentencing is best used with nonviolent offenders who have few prior arrests and little or no history of imprisonment.
   a. True*
   b. False

5. Many offenders find intermediate sanctions more punishing than imprisonment.
   a. True*
   b. False

6. Restitution, in all its forms, carries with it elements of deterrence and retribution.
   a. True*
   b. False

7. Retribution requires offenders to repay victims or the community for the material and financial costs of their crimes.
   a. True
   b. False*

8. Persons convicted of crimes in which there is no identifiable complainant except the state can make restitution by performing community service.
   a. True*
   b. False

9. Officers handling ISP caseloads have fewer clients than other officers and spend more time monitoring each client's activities.
   a. True*
   b. False

10. Intensive supervision clients are so closely watched that they rarely face revocation for technical violations.
    a. True
    b. False*

11. Although it costs more than prison, intensive supervision is more likely to reduce recidivism than imprisonment.
    a. True
    b. False*

12. "Specialized caseloads" almost always receive intensive supervision.
    a. True*
    b. False

13. Therapeutic communities accepting probated clients use some coercive elements, but do not physically prevent clients from escaping.
    a. True*
    b. False

14. People in the United States are the most monitored in the world today.
    a. True*
    b. False

15. Some fear that intermediate sanctions will make community supervision so popular that many people will come under correctional control who do not need supervision.
    a. True*
    b. False

Essay and Discussion Items

1. How do liberals and conservatives feel about intermediate sanctions? Why?

2. For what kinds of offenders are intermediate sanctions designed?

3. Compare restitution and community service. List their similarities and differences.

4. What are the advantages of Intensive Supervision Programs (ISPs)? What problems do they pose?

5. What types of people would be found at a day center? What advantages do day centers offer? Why are there so few of them?

6. What are the goals of a boot camp? A therapeutic community? What are the limitations of each?

7. What factors must be taken into consideration in evaluating the effectiveness of intermediate sanctions?

8. What dangers are posed by the use of intermediate sanctions?

Chapter Six

Post-Imprisonment Community Supervision

Learning Objectives

1. Distinguish parole from probation and from alternative methods of release from prison.
2. Describe the various methods by which parole may be granted and describe the release process.
3. Describe the legal bases of parole and relate these to the rights of releasees and parole officers.
4. Discuss the composition and powers of the parole board.
5. List the factors that predict post-release recidivism.
6. List the differences in procedures between parole and probation revocation.
7. Identify the basic types of parole officers.
8. Summarize the issues that characterize officer-releasee relations and describe their practical and ethical implications.

Chapter Outline

Comparison of Probation and Parole
Methods of Release from Prison
    Unconditional and Conditional Releases
    Discretionary Release
    Pardons
    Mandatory Discharge
    Mandatory Release
    Parole
Goals of Parole
The Legal Bases of Parole
    Theories of Grace, Custody, and Contract
The Organization of Paroling Authorities

Major Points

1. Most prisoners will reenter society but this may occur with or without supervision and may be legislatively mandated or a matter of executive discretion.

2. Parole officers supervise more serious offenders than probation officers and releasees have also been hardened by the experience of imprisonment.

3. Parole is legally justified by the theories of grace and continuing custody.

4. Parole boards have traditionally been accountable to no one but are increasingly being forced to use objective criteria and rationally support their decisions.

5. Recidivism is predicted by long sentences, reliance on crime for an income, youth, education, and other factors but the prediction problem remains severe and the correctional mission inevitably involves risk taking by authorities.

6. Parole supervision and revocation are guided by similar principles and court decisions but parole boards and hearing officers replace judges in the parole revocation process.

7. Parole and probation officers may be punitive, welfare-oriented, passive, and lazy or paternal in style. The latter is preferred because it applies both control and support as indicated by the offender's behavior.

8. Officers and releasees come from different social worlds and have different ideas about what constitutes "success." Officers must always remember that they are in a power relationship with their clients and this places both ethical and clinical limits on their activities.

Key Terms

Commutation of sentence
Conditional release
Continuing custody
Discretionary release
Dual relationship
Executive clemency
Mandatory discharge

Mandatory supervised release
Pardon
Parole
Release plan
Street time
Theory of grace
Unconditional release

Chapter Summary

Most prison inmates will eventually be released back into society but the method by which they are released is determined by law. The discretion of the parole board is often involved in release decisions but mandatory release and mandatory discharge are becoming more popular as well. Pardons are rare and may be conditional or unconditional. Parole and mandatory release are conditional forms of release in which the offender is supervised by a parole officer according to conditions set by a parole board. Legally, parole is a privilege in which the state retains theoretical custody but permits the offender to live in the community. Parole board members are appointed by the governor and decide which inmates will be released early, the conditions of release, and which ones should have their liberty revoked. Parole may be denied to facilitate virtually any correctional goal and parole boards have not traditionally had to explain their actions to anyone. However, many states are trying to cut litigation costs by use of objective criteria in parole decisions. Release from prison should be a gradual and planned process in which prison and parole authorities cooperate. Although the process of parole supervision is similar to that of probation, recidivism is more common and revocation is handled by special officers rather than a judge. The chapter offers a typology of community supervision officers that rates their focus on both control and support. Also discussed are the main factors that guide the client-officer relationship. Readers are warned against the ethical and practical dangers of dual relationships for those employed in corrections.

Examination Questions

Multiple Choice Items

1. People under supervision after being released from prison differ from probationers in that:
   a. they were among the most serious offenders in their communities.
   b. they found it hard to adapt to the community supervision prior to prison and had their probation revoked.

c. prison taught them to distrust others and solve problems with deceit or violence.

d. any or all of the above.*

2. Being a convicted felon affects a person's _____ for the rest of their life.

a. identity

b. social status

c. material welfare

d. all of the above*

3. Which of the following is a method by which an inmate might be released from prison?

a. pardon

b. conditional mandatory release

c. unconditional mandatory discharge

d. parole

e. all of the above*

4. Both parole and supervised mandatory release are _____ forms of release.

a. conditional*

b. lenient

c. stringent

d. unconditional

5. Offenders who are not supervised after prison are said to have received a(n) _____ release.

a. conditional

b. lenient

c. stringent

d. unconditional*

6. Commutations and pardons are both forms of:

a. lenient sentencing.

b. executive clemency.*

c. judicial reprieves.

d. legislative forgiveness.

7. The most common type of unconditional release is _____, which infers that the offender did not qualify for discretionary release or good time.

a. parole

b. gubernatorial pardon

c. mandatory discharge*

d. presidential pardon

8. _____ occurs when an offender has served the maximum sentence assigned by the trial court minus good time.

a. Mandatory supervised release*

b. Parole

    c. Pardon

    d. Mandatory discharge

9. Parole allows the criminal justice system to:

    a. supervise the offender after he has been released from prison.

    b. advertise severe sanctions while quietly alleviating overcrowding and financial pressures in prisons.

    c. even out sentencing disparities.

    d. all of the above.

    e. a and b only.*

10. Legally, parole is a:

    a. right.

    b. matter of contract.

    c. privilege.*

    d. all of the above.

11. Parole is:

    a. supervision in the community following imprisonment.

    b. a privilege extended to inmates by the legislature or parole board.

    c. a method of encouraging inmates to follow prison rules.

    d. a period of adjustment to free society following imprisonment.

    e. all of the above.*

12. A parole board is usually appointed by:

    a. the legislature.

    b. the governor.*

    c. the Supreme Court or Court of Criminal Appeals.

    d. the Department of Corrections.

13. To be appointed to a parole board, most states require that one have:

    a. a degree in criminal justice or abnormal psychology.

    b. five years experience in the justice system.

    c. the nomination of the governor.*

    d. all of the above.

14. The responsibilities of a parole board usually include:

    a. setting the policies that determine which inmates will receive discretionary release.

    b. setting the conditions of release for each offender.

    c. deciding which offenders should be revoked.

    d. advising the governor and legislature on matters related to the reintegration of offenders and public safety.

    e. all of the above.*

15. It is increasingly common to see parole boards using _____ criteria based on factors that have been found to predict success among parolees in the past to grant paroles.

    a. actuarial*

    b. clinical

    c. subjective

    d. anamnestic

16. Parole is typical of the entire correctional enterprise because it relies on:

    a. popular support for leniency.

    b. the logic of the justice model.

    c. estimates of the danger of recidivism.*

    d. the judgement of elected officials.

17. Which of the following rights does an inmate have when his parole is being considered?

    a. notice of the hearing.

    b. right to present evidence and confront accusers.

    c. right to an attorney.

    d. all of the above.*

18. A release plan:

    a. describes where the offender will live and work after release.

    b. is checked out by a parole officer in the field.

    c. can be rejected or modified by field officers.

    d. is all of the above.*

19. Conditions of parole are assigned by:

    a. the parole officer.

    b. the prison warden.

    c. the parole board.*

    d. the local police chief or sheriff.

20. An inmate may be released due to action taken by:

    a. the legislature.

    b. the governor.

    c. the parole board.

    d. any of the above.*

21. Which of the following may be used to justify special conditions of release from prison?

    a. past offenses.

    b. arrests that did not lead to a conviction.

    c. disciplinary problems in the prison.

    d. all of the above.*

22. One out of every _____ releasees who are revoked have violated only a technical condition of release rather than having committed a new crime.

    a. two

    b. three*

    c. five

    d. ten

23. Approximately _____ percent of those granted conditional release from prison complete their sentence successfully in the community.
    a. ten
    b. forty
    c. sixty*
    d. eighty

24. Parole may be (and often is) denied because:
    a. the convict has not adjusted to the institutional lifestyle.
    b. the parole board feels the inmate is a threat to public safety.
    c. of boundary-setting and general deterrence needs that are not directly related to the inmate.
    d. correctional authorities have not yet assessed the risks and needs of the inmate.
    e. all of the above.*

25. Which of the following does NOT predict success for a parolee?
    a. being older (over 45).
    b. having a short criminal record.
    c. conviction for a "non-vocational" offense.
    d. serving a long sentence.*

26. The most serious problems faced by ex-prisoners center on their:
    a. ability to get a job.*
    b. loss of social skills while imprisoned.
    c. hatred of society.
    d. inevitable return to crime.

27. A program that helps releasees get jobs and obtain counseling will save _____ for each dollar it spends.
    a. one dollar
    b. four dollars*
    c. twenty dollars
    d. one hundred dollars

28. Opponents of laws that require public notification when sex offenders are present in the community fear each of the following EXCEPT:
    a. the civil rights of the offender will be violated.*
    b. parents will develop a false sense of safety.
    c. vigilantism will result.
    d. social isolation and stress will drive these offenders to commit new crimes.

29. Revocation of parole usually involves _____ hearings before a neutral party.
    a. two*
    b. three
    c. five
    d. ten

30. An absconder is a probationer or parolee who has:
    a. committed a crime while under supervision.
    b. hidden from the supervising officer.
    c. committed only a minor technical violation.*
    d. cooperated fully with authorities.

31. _____ time is the portion of the sentence served under parole supervision that can be lost as a result of revocation.
    a. Good
    b. Street*
    c. Free
    d. Down

32. Many states use _____ to conduct parole revocation hearings and make recommendations to the parole board.
    a. legislative committees
    b. hearing officers*
    c. retired judges
    d. parole supervisors

33. Which of the following is NOT true of revocation of probation/parole:
    a. violating any criminal law can result in revocation.
    b. violating the conditions of release can result in revocation.
    c. the majority of available evidence must indicate guilt.
    d. the offender must be proven guilty beyond a reasonable doubt.*

34. The paternal role is preferred by the author because it:
    a. emphasizes treatment.
    b. emphasizes control.
    c. can do either or both of the above.*
    d. does neither of the above.

35. The preferred type of parole/probation officer is described as a:
    a. punitive officer.
    b. welfare worker.
    c. paternal officer.*
    d. passive agent.

36. A _____ focuses on punishment and control.
    a. punitive officer*
    b. welfare worker
    c. paternal officer
    d. passive agent

37. A _____ focuses on assisting the offender in building a happy, productive life. They often presume that happy people do not commit crimes.
    a. punitive officer
    b. welfare worker*

c. paternal officer
d. passive agent

38. A parole officer who likes having a secure government job but avoids any task that will require much effort is known as a:
   a. punitive officer.
   b. welfare worker.
   c. paternal officer.
   d. passive agent.*

39. Relationships between parole/probation officers and the offenders they supervise are guided by the fact that:
   a. the officer is trying to "convert" the offender to conventional life.
   b. the offender seeks survival with dignity.
   c. the officer has the power to revoke liberty.
   d. all of the above.*

40. A parole officer allowing a releasee to fix her car would be an example of a:
   a. bribe.
   b. dual relationship.*
   c. criminal act.
   d. legitimate job benefit.

True-False Items

1. The stigma of being a convicted felon affects a person's identity, social status, and material welfare for the rest of their life.
   a. True*
   b. False

2. Pardons are granted by the legislature after a recommendation from the parole board.
   a. True
   b. False*

3. Mandatory releasees are released to supervision for the length of the good time they have earned in prison.
   a. True*
   b. False

4. Persons who receive a mandatory discharge from custody behaved so poorly in prison that they did not earn any good time.
   a. True*
   b. False

5. The decision to grant parole may be discretionary or legislatively mandated.
   a. True*
   b. False

6. The granting of parole is always a matter of choice for the parole board.
    a. True
    b. False*

7. Conditions of parole may reflect past offenses as well as those for which the person was actually imprisoned.
    a. True*
    b. False

8. One out of every three releasees who are revoked have violated only a technical condition of release rather than having committed a new crime.
    a. True*
    b. False

9. Sixty percent of those granted conditional release from prison complete their sentence successfully in the community.
    a. True*
    b. False

10. In some states the parole officer is empowered to arrest a releasee for whom a warrant has been issued.
    a. True*
    b. False

11. Releasees have a right to bail and other forms of release from jail prior to their revocation hearing.
    a. True
    b. False*

12. At least one out of every five parolees is an absconder.
    a. True
    b. False*

13. "Street time" is the portion of the sentence served under parole supervision that can be lost as a result of revocation.
    a. True*
    b. False

14. Releasees have the same rights in a revocation hearing as in a criminal trial.
    a. True
    b. False*

15. The preferred role of the parole officer is described as paternal and uses a mixture of control and support that is determined by the attitude and behavior of each releasee.
    a. True*
    b. False

Essay and Discussion Items

1. Compare parole and probation in terms of the kinds of people supervised, the methods of supervision used, and the legal bases of each type of supervision.

2. List and describe the ways by which an offender may be legally released from prison.

3. What legal ideas lie at the root of parole? How do these ideas affect the powers of parole officers and parole boards?

4. How is a parole board composed and what are its powers?

5. Through what steps should an inmate pass in the process of being released?

6. What factors predict post-release recidivism?

7. Describe the four basic orientations of parole/probation officers and evaluate each in terms of how well it meets the goals of community supervision.

8. To what issues should a parole officer be sensitive while dealing with releasees? What types of conduct should be encouraged or avoided? Why?

Chapter Seven

Prison Populations

Learning Objectives

1. Compare current U.S. imprisonment rates with those of the last 75 years and those of other nations.
2. Describe the composition of U.S. prison populations and list the issues involved in disproportionate minority confinement rates.
3. Compare the quantity and traits of inmates in federal and state systems.
4. Describe the impact of AIDS and TB on prisons and the steps used to control these and other diseases.
5. Identify the categories included in the term "special needs offenders," describe the unique problems encountered by each, and discuss institutional responses to them.
6. Identify the reason for and challenges presented by the aging of the inmate population.
7. Define correctional classification and its subtypes as well as identify its goals and methods.

Chapter Outline

The Growth of U.S. Imprisonment Rates
Prisoner Traits
    Racial Imbalances in U.S. Imprisonment Patterns
U.S. Inmates: Traits and Trends
Federal and State Systems
Prisoner Health Issues
    HIV/AIDS
      Prevention Efforts
    Tuberculosis
Special Needs Offenders
    The Mentally Disabled
    The Physically Disabled

Aging Offenders
   Unique Traits of Older Inmates
Drug Abusers
Sex Offenders
Correctional Classification
   Types
   Goals
Summary

Major Points

1. U.S. prison populations are growing at an unprecedented rate: the U.S. rate of imprisonment is second only to that of Russia and has seen more growth in the last two decades than ever before.

2. Minorities are grossly over-represented among prisoners and this imbalance is increasing largely because of the way in which the war on drugs is being waged.

3. Federal and state systems differ in the nature and traits of the inmates they hold.

4. Because HIV/AIDS and TB are very common among inmates, prisons are excellent places to educate large numbers of people in high-risk categories. Testing programs are available but confinement contributes to the spread of these diseases.

5. "Special needs offenders" include the mentally and physically disabled, aging inmates, drug abusers, and sex offenders. Each group has unique problems and poses a different sort of challenge to correctional authorities.

6. Correctional classification occurs at the systemic and institutional levels as prisons try to use past behavior and psychological profiles to prevent problems before they occur.

Key Terms

American with Disabilities Act (ADA)	Psychological classification
Correctional classification	Rate of imprisonment
The "count"	Risk-oriented classification
HIV/AIDS	Segregation units
Institutional classification	Special needs offenders
Multiculturalism	System-wide classification

Chapter Summary

The U.S. has the second highest rate of imprisonment in the industrialized world and the highest rate of violence. Rates of confinement have grown more dramatically in the last twenty-five years than at any other time. Violence, intolerance for probation/parole violations, and the war on drugs are the causes of this growth. However, the growing discrepancy in confinement rates between minorities and whites is due primarily to the war on drugs; violence within minority communities may receive more lenient treatment than that affecting whites. Both federal and state systems are affected by these trends despite the fact that they hold qualitatively different groups of offenders: federal inmates have higher IQs, are more often drug law violators, and are less often from the inner city than those in state facilities. Drug use and other aspects of inmates' lifestyles result in especially high rates of AIDS, TB, and other serious diseases as well as premature aging. These factors are forcing prisons to use education and testing to reduce the spread of disease but some measures, like condom distribution, are avoided for moral reasons. Elderly offenders and the disabled present special financial and clinical challenges to authorities and the number of such inmates will increase in the future. Dealing with the problems of these inmates will require sensitivity and creativity as well as financial investments. These inmates are especially susceptible to attacks and harassment by fellow inmates. Correctional classification is a traditional method of preventing problems among inmates that is of only limited use in addressing the needs of the aging and disabled. However, it is a vital method of bureaucratic control which is based on past behavior and/or psychological predictions.

Examination Questions

Multiple Choice Items

1. Which of the following is expected to have a significant impact on the size and nature of correctional populations?
   a. general social trends, like the aging of the nation's population.
   b. changes in the criminal law.
   c. changes in government priorities.
   d. the problems of the poor.
   e. all of the above.*

2. Which of the following has a rate of imprisonment that is higher than that of the United States?
   a. England
   b. Russia*
   c. Israel
   d. South Africa
   e. all of the above

3. Which of the following has a higher rate of violence than the United States?
    a. Canada
    b. Russia
    c. China
    d. none of the above*

4. Economists warn that the current rate of imprisonment could soon lead to:
    a. a serious lack of qualified correctional workers.
    b. economic disaster for many states.*
    c. a hyperactive economy.
    d. all of the above.

5. Nobel Prize winners are predicting that:
    a. growing rates of imprisonment could lead to bankruptcy.*
    b. hiring by the prison industry is reducing unemployment.
    c. large cities will become unmanageable if we fail to imprison most law-breakers.
    d. all of the above.

6. Overall, economists point out that prisons:
    a. contribute many high-paying jobs to the nation's economy.
    b. do less for the economy than virtually any other sort of activity.*
    c. have no effect on the economy.
    d. have never been examined scientifically.

7. Most of the inmates of _____ facilities have been convicted of a violent offense.
    a. state*
    b. federal
    c. county
    d. city

8. Federal prisoners are more often _____ than are state inmates.
    a. white collar offenders
    b. drug couriers or "mules"
    c. higher in IQ
    d. all of the above*

9. Most _____ inmates have been convicted of a drug offense.
    a. state
    b. federal*
    c. county
    d. city

10. In general, prison inmates tend to be:
    a. substance abusers.
    b. unemployed.
    c. unmarried.
    d. all of the above.*

11. Most prison inmates are:
    a. from large cities.
    b. under 40 years of age.
    c. males.
    d. minorities.
    e. all of the above.*

12. Which of the following is NOT a result of rising imprisonment rates?
    a. Other services, like education, are getting a smaller share of state funding.
    b. Drug use is being reduced throughout the nation*.
    c. Unemployment rates are artificially suppressed.
    d. Victims feel that justice is being better served.

13. The rate of incarceration for African-American males is approximately _____ times greater than that for whites.
    a. 2
    b. 8*
    c. 20
    d. 100

14. Racial imbalances in prison populations _____ as rates of imprisonment rise.
    a. become more extreme*
    b. become less extreme
    c. are unaffected
    d. cease to exist

15. The increase in the overall rate of imprisonment is due to:
    a. decreased tolerance for violence.
    b. the war on drugs.
    c. decreased tolerance for probation and parole violations.
    d. all of the above.*

16. The increase in the rate of imprisonment for African Americans is due to:
    a. decreased tolerance for violence.
    b. the war on drugs.*
    c. decreased tolerance for probation and parole violations.
    d. all of the above.

17. Throughout history, imprisonment patterns have been most strongly impacted by the:
    a. nature and extent of crime.
    b. type of government.
    c. economic power structure of the society.*
    d. all of the above.

18. The high rate of HIV among male prison populations is due mainly to the fact that many:
    a. lived in unsanitary conditions prior to imprisonment.

b. were active homosexuals.

c. worked as prostitutes.

d. were intravenous drug users.*

19. The primary response to AIDS in prisons is:

    a. isolation of at-risk inmates.

    b. testing and education.*

    c. sterilization.

    d. medical experimentation.

20. Most U.S. prisons now test inmates for AIDS:

    a. upon admission to prison.

    b. if they belong to high risk groups or request it.*

    c. if they are suspected of prior promiscuity.

    d. all of the above.

21. The proportion of inmates infected with HIV/AIDS is increasing the fastest among:

    a. whites.

    b. African Americans.

    c. males.

    d. females.*

22. The leading cause of death among prison inmates is:

    a. AIDS.

    b. natural causes.*

    c. murder.

    d. suicide.

23. Inmates are at high risk for tuberculosis because:

    a. they are drug/alcohol abusers and/or HIV-positive.

    b. they are poor and/or minorities.

    c. confinement and crowding increase the risk of TB infection.

    d. all of the above.*

24. Tuberculosis is about _____ times more common among inmates than the general population.

    a. 2

    b. 5*

    c. 10

    d. 100

25. The _____ requires that all disabled citizens have access to public facilities and be given all possible opportunities to lead productive lives.

    a. Civil Rights Act of 1871

    b. Civil Rights Act of 1964

    c. Prison Litigation Reform Act

    d. Americans with Disabilities Act*

26. Handling the needs of the physically disabled is a matter of:

a. creativity and sensitivity.
b. architecture and funding.
c. both of the above.*
d. neither of the above.

27. The term "Special Needs Offenders" includes:

    a. the mentally challenged.
    b. those with serious mental disorders.
    c. substance abusers.
    d. sex offenders.
    e. all of the above.*

28. Illegal drugs are _____ to obtain in most U.S. prisons.

    a. easy*
    b. hard
    c. impossible
    d. cheap

29. _____ is the only drug recognized by the U.S. Justice Department as known to cause aggression in humans and is a factor in about 60% of homicides.

    a. Cocaine
    b. Marijuana
    c. Heroin
    d. Alcohol*

30. When compared with other inmates, sex offenders tend to be:

    a. older.
    b. less often part of a criminal subculture.
    c. easier to control.
    d. all of the above.*
    e. none of the above.

31. Scientific studies show that about _____ % of sex offenders commit further sex crimes after release from prison.

    a. 20*
    b. 40
    c. 75
    d. 90

32. Sex offenders have _____ rates of post-imprisonment re-offending than do drug or violent offenders.

    a. higher
    b. similar
    c. equal
    d. lower*

33. Inmates with mental disabilities serious enough to assure them treatment include each of the following EXCEPT those who:
    a. are so disturbed that they cannot control their thoughts, actions, or emotions.
    b. are so retarded that they cannot adapt to the demands of the institution.
    c. are at risk for suicide.
    d. have personality disorders.*

34. Most elderly inmates:
    a. are sex offenders.
    b. committed crimes early in life and received long sentences.*
    c. are large scale drug traffickers or white collar criminals.
    d. are all of the above.

35. Penologists define inmates over the age of _____ as older or elderly.
    a. 40
    b. 55*
    c. 65
    d. 75

36. _____ uses estimates of the threat posed by each inmate to assign prisoners to specific facilities.
    a. Institutional classification
    b. Regional assessment
    c. System wide classification*
    d. All of the above

37. _____ is done later to place inmates in specific housing areas, programs, and work assignments.
    a. Institutional classification*
    b. Regional assessment
    c. System wide classification
    d. All of the above

38. Which of the following is the predominant concern in the classification process?
    a. rehabilitation
    b. costs
    c. discipline*
    d. all of the above are of equal concern

39. _____ classification systems focus on the security issues raised by the offender's background, legal history, and personality.
    a. Psychological
    b. Risk-based*
    c. Institutional
    d. System wide

40. _____ are special long-term, close-confinement areas for inmates who are at high risk of escape or violence which constitute the most secure facilities in use today.

    a. Isolation pods
    b. Solitary confinement cells
    c. Segregation units*
    d. Star chambers

True-False Items

1. The U.S. has the second highest rate of imprisonment in the industrialized world.

    a. True*
    b. False

2. The costs of imprisonment are too small to have any effect on the economy according to most experts.

    a. True
    b. False*

3. Economists warn that the current rate of imprisonment could lead to economic disaster in the near future.

    a. True*
    b. False

4. The text identifies a cycle in which low wages lead to crime and imprisonment which further lower earnings and thus encourage even more crime.

    a. True*
    b. False

5. Because most serious violence occurs in minority neighborhoods, violence against minorities is treated much more severely than violence which victimizes whites.

    a. True
    b. False*

6. Throughout history, imprisonment patterns have reflected the economic power structure of the society more than its crime problem.

    a. True*
    b. False

7. Tuberculosis is much more common in jails and prisons than in the mainstream society.

    a. True*
    b. False

8. Most prisons separate HIV-positive inmates from the general inmate population as soon as they are identified.
   a. True
   b. False*

9. Most U.S. prisons allow distribution of condoms to inmates.
   a. True
   b. False*

10. Sex offenders have lower re-offense rates than do drug or violent offenders.
    a. True*
    b. False

11. Aging offenders are so few in number that they pose little threat to prison budgets.
    a. True
    b. False*

12. Disabled offenders pose little threat to prison budgets.
    a. True*
    b. False

13. As the average age of inmates in a facility increases, the rate of disciplinary problems drops.
    a. True*
    b. False

14. It is cheaper to keep older inmates in prison once they become ill than to place them in nursing homes.
    a. True
    b. False*

15. Correctional classification is designed mainly to meet the treatment needs of each inmate.
    a. True
    b. False*

Essay and Discussion Items

1. What trends characterize U.S. prison populations? What are the causes of these trends? Who is most affected by them?

2. Discuss the pros and cons of using deterrence to reduce violence in impoverished minority communities. What factors are most important in addressing this issue?

3. Do U.S. imprisonment rates reflect the true nature of the crime problem or merely long-standing social prejudices? What facts support your position? Which contradict it?

4. How do the inmate populations of federal and state prisons differ? What factors account for these differences?

5. What are the chief health issues confronting modern prisons? How is each being dealt with by authorities?

6. What is meant by the term "special needs offenders"? What groups are included in this category? What problems does each face?

7. Why is the prison population gradually growing older? What are the characteristics of older inmates? What problems do they pose for current and future prison policies?

8. What is correctional classification? What purposes does it serve? What forms does it take?

Chapter Eight

Convict Society

Learning Objectives

1. Contrast deprivation theory with importation theory and discuss which aspects of prison life are best explained by each approach.

2. Define "total institution" and describe the effects of such a facility on the behavior of its inmates.

3. Distinguish between prosocial, antisocial, pseudo-social, and asocial orientations among inmates.

4. List the major prison gangs in the U.S., discuss their activities, and describe the threats they pose to prison security.

5. Describe the informal economy of convict society.

6. List the factors that predict prison violence.

7. Discuss what research shows about the sexual behavior of male inmates. Distinguish between situational and dispositional homosexuality.

8. Describe the overall impact of imprisonment on offenders and recidivism rates.

Chapter Outline

Explanations of Convict Society
    Importation Theory
    Deprivation Theory
The Total Institution
    Prisonization
Types of Prisoners
Prison Gangs
Special Issues in Prison Life
    The Informal Economy of the Prison
    Prison Violence
    Sexual Behavior in Prison
Summary

Major Points

1. Some aspects of prison life result from factors imported from criminal subcultures in the free world; others are produced by the deprivations of imprisonment and related situational factors.

2. Prisons, by their nature, are total institutions which make inmates less fit to live in society by increasing their exposure to criminal norms, forcing them to live in a violent setting and relieving them of ordinary responsibilities.

3. The degree to which inmates are "prisonized" varies with their personality, their choices of recreation and companions, and the length of their sentence.

4. Prisoners' relations with staff and the outside world can be described in terms of four basic orientations: prosocial, antisocial, pseudo-social, and asocial.

5. Prison gangs coexist with street and biker gangs, their membership is race-based, and they are responsible for much of the serious violence and drug traffic within prisons.

6. Prisoners barter a wide variety of goods and services in an attempt to overcome some of the deprivations of incarceration.

7. The younger the average age of inmates in a facility, and the more recidivists present, the greater the likelihood of high rates of prison violence.

8. Some inmates are bi- or homosexual by disposition; others engage in consensual or coerced sex as a situational homosexuality to cope with the prison environment.

Key Terms

Conjugal visits
Degradation ceremonies
Deprivation theory
Dispositional homosexuality
Furlough
Importation theory
Learned helplessness

Prisonization
Situational factors
Situational homosexuality
State-raised youth
Time horizon
Total institution
Wheeler's U-curve

Chapter Highlights

The daily routines and status roles of prison inmates are shaped by varying combinations of imported factors and situational deprivations. Because they are total institutions, prisons reinforce learned helplessness, present-oriented thinking, and a lack of accountability among inmates. Prisonization is a function of many factors, but length of sentence, personality, decisions about deviant opportunities, and choice of associates are powerful predictors of the degree of institutionalization a particular inmate will experience. Along with social learning and constant fear of violence, prisonization makes inmates less able to live productive lives than before incarceration. Prison gangs are racially based and make a large contribution to the violence and drug abuse found in most prisons. Prisoners use an informal, barter economy to overcome some of the deprivations of imprisonment. Violence is endemic to prison life and results from combinations of situational and imported factors. Research on inmate sexual behavior shows mixed and even contradictory results but coerced homosexuality, if not outright rape, is common in many institutions.

Examination Questions

Multiple Choice Items

1. _____ asserts that status roles and subcultures of the prison are products of the identities established by inmates before imprisonment.
   a. Deprivation theory
   b. The labeling perspective
   c. Importation theory*
   d. The conflict perspective

2. Which of the following is the most recent addition to the variety of subcultures found in U.S. prisons?
   a. the thief subculture of property offenders
   b. the professional criminal subculture of offenders with specialized criminal skills
   c. the Pepsi Generation subculture of violent, gang-involved inmates*
   d. the conventional subculture who follow the larger society's norms

3. _____ alleges that inmate societies develop out of the hardships suffered by inmates while incarcerated.
   a. Deprivation theory*
   b. The labeling perspective
   c. Importation theory
   d. The conflict perspective

4. In penology, a **situational** factor is one that:
   a. is brought into the prison by inmates from their home communities.
   b. occurs as a result of the organization of prison life.*
   c. occurs only occasionally as a result of unusual circumstances.
   d. all of the above.

5. A(n) _____ is a bureaucratically administered facility in which a large number of people with similar statuses live for relatively long periods of time with little contact with the outside world.
   a. total institution*

   b. open facility
   c. closed facility
   d. partial institution

6. The acquisition, to lesser or greater degree, of the general culture of the penitentiary is called:
   a. enculturation.
   b. assimilation.
   c. criminogenesis.
   d. prisonization.*

7. Which of the following is NOT true of the conclusions reached by Zimbardo after experimenting with college students?
   a. prisons create and/or worsen pathology in both guards and inmates.
   b. prisons should be reserved for only the most dangerous offenders.
   c. prisons can rehabilitate offenders if run democratically so that inmates control their environment.*
   d. all of the above ARE true of Zimbardo's conclusions.

8. Wheeler's U-curve thesis is based on research showing that:
   a. inmate attitudes are more antisocial at the beginning of their sentence than at the end.
   b. inmate attitudes are most prosocial during the first and last six months of their sentence.*
   c. inmate attitudes are more antisocial at the end of their sentence than at the beginning.
   d. there is no relationship between an inmate's attitude and how much of his sentence had been served.

9. Which of the following would NOT minimize prisonization?
   a. a short sentence.
   b. positive relationships with non-criminals outside the prison.
   c. avoiding deviant activities while imprisoned.
   d. having a stable personality.
   e. all of the above ARE factors that would minimize prisonization.*

10. An inmate with much knowledge of, and many contacts in, both the prison and outside world but little loyalty to either is referred to as having a(n) _____ orientation.
   a. prosocial.
   b. antisocial.
   c. pseudosocial.*
   d. asocial.

11. Which of the following orientations best exemplifies the norms of the convict code:
   a. prosocial
   b. antisocial*

c. pseudo-social
d. asocial

12. Once an offender has experienced prison life, its deterrent value for him is most likely to:

    a. increase slightly.
    b. increase greatly.
    c. remain the same.
    d. decrease.*

13. When a person prefers relationships with the opposite sex but resorts to homosexual liaisons when forced into a sexually segregated living situation, the resulting behavior is called _____ homosexuality.

    a. prisonized
    b. dispositional
    c. situational*
    d. socialized

14. Prisonization:

    a. consists mainly of learning how to enjoy prison life.
    b. deters crime and helps achieve restitution.
    c. socializes inmates to accept the identity and subcultural norms of convict society.*
    d. is predicted largely by imported variables.

15. The idea of being powerless to affect one's own life, depending on others for virtually everything and blaming others for what happens is known as:

    a. prisonization.
    b. deprivation response.
    c. learned helplessness.*
    d. none of the above.

16. Which of the following is a major cause of prisonization?

    a. involuntary incarceration.
    b. segregation from mainstream society, significant others, and the opposite sex.
    c. the complex, unique system of social roles in prison.
    d. degradation ceremonies.
    e. all of the above are major sources of prisonization.*

17. Which of the following is NOT likely to minimize prisonization?

    a. serving time in a small, treatment-oriented facility.
    b. high levels of security.*
    c. having a stable personality.
    d. rejecting the norms of the convict society.
    e. avoiding deviant activities within the prison.

18. _____ is the preferred drug among prison inmates who use drugs.
    a. Heroin*
    b. Cocaine
    c. Marijuana
    d. Ecstasy

19. _____ is a person's ability to examine the future consequences of actions being considered in the present and is an important predictor of crime.
    a. Verbal IQ
    b. Catastrophisizing
    c. Time horizon*
    d. All of the above

20. Murderers are often of the _____ type.
    a. prosocial*
    b. antisocial
    c. pseudo-social
    d. asocial

21. Which of the following is NOT one of the two biggest problems facing prison officials in the 1990s?
    a. crowding
    b. gangs
    c. court intervention*
    d. all of the above are of equal concern in the 1990s.

22. Prison gangs first appeared in the _____ .
    a. 1800s
    b. 1920s
    c. 1950s*
    d. 1980s

23. The _____ is the largest white prison gang.
    a. Aryan Brotherhood*
    b. Ku Klux Klan
    c. White Aryan Resistance
    d. Hammerskins

24. Prison gangs are organized according to the _____ of their inmate-members.
    a. offense
    b. hometown
    c. race*
    d. social role

25. Prison gangs are:
    a. easily infiltrated by authorities.
    b. hard to penetrate or learn about.*

   c. something members brag openly about.

   d. a source of financial support for their members.

26. Inmates may obtain desired items and services:

   a. as gifts from friends and relatives in free society.

   b. from the prison canteen or commissary.

   c. through smuggling by staff and visitors.

   d. by stealing and making items within the prison.

   e. all of the above.*

27. Inmate knives are usually:

   a. made within the prison.*

   b. intended for attacks on staff.

   c. obtained from visitors.

   d. constructed for use in escapes.

28. The informal inmate economy is:

   a. a violation of prison rules.

   b. based on barter.

   c. vital to the operation of convict society.

   d. all of the above.*

29. In the inmate economy:

   a. cigarettes and other items are used instead of money.

   b. most transactions between inmates are a rule violation.

   c. violence is used to collect debts and settle disputes.

   d. all of the above.*

30. Staff and visitors are persuaded to smuggle contraband as a result of:

   a. bribes.

   b. blackmail.

   c. threats.

   d. all of the above.*

31. Official objections to the hidden economy of convict society focus on the idea that:

   a. weapons, drugs, and alcohol move through the prison because of the inmate economy.

   b. it threatens the ability of authorities to control the rewards of prison life.

   c. dissatisfaction with the goods purchased often leads to violence.

   d. all of the above.*

32. The American Correctional Association believes that _____ are the main causes of prison riots.

   a. enforced idleness

   b. lack of meaningful programs

   c. unpredictable or severe parole policies

   d. inhumane treatment and overcrowding

   e. all of the above.*

33. The causes of prison riots are:
    a. imported.
    b. situational.*
    c. escape attempts.
    d. all of the above.

34. Interpersonal violence among inmates is due largely to _____ factors.
    a. imported*
    b. situational
    c. escape attempts
    d. all of the above

35. _____ is/are the primary form of sexual release in prison.
    a. Masturbation*
    b. Rape
    c. Prostitution
    d. Conjugal visits

36. _____ homosexuality means that an individual prefers partners of the same sex.
    a. Symbiotic
    b. Dispositional*
    c. Situational
    d. Inadvertent

37. Homosexuals are usually segregated from other inmates in order to:
    a. discourage prostitution.
    b. prevent them from committing rapes.
    c. protect them from rape.*
    d. avoid social learning of such behavior by other inmates.

38. _____ visits give prisoners the opportunity for unsupervised social and sexual contacts with their spouses within the prison.
    a. Conjugal *
    b. Emergency medical
    c. Parental
    d. Parole

39. Conjugal visits are accepted in much of:
    a. the United States.
    b. western Europe.*
    c. Asia.
    d. Africa.

40. _____ makes inmates less able to live in society than they were prior to being imprisoned and retards efforts toward rehabilitation.
    a. Deterrence
    b. Reintegration
    c. Prisonization*
    d. All of the above

True-False Items

1. Deprivation theory asserts that status roles and subcultures of the prison are products of the identities established by inmates before imprisonment.
   a. True
   b. False*

2. Inmates tend to stick together regardless of their offense or background.
   a. True
   b. False*

3. The Pepsi Generation is a traditional and well-respected prison subculture.
   a. True
   b. False*

4. Deprivation theory alleges that inmate societies develop out of the hardships suffered by inmates while incarcerated.
   a. True*
   b. False

5. Examination of changes in the "convict code" since the 1950s show that prison life is more violent than ever before.
   a. True*
   b. False

6. The process of prisonization affects only inmates.
   a. True
   b. False*

7. Prisonization is the most effective deterrent to recidivism available today.
   a. True
   b. False*

8. In general, the more control an institution exerts over inmates, the more negative its impact on post-release behavior.
   a. True*
   b. False

9. Changes designed to reduce prisonization would also be perceived as reducing the amount of punishment associated with imprisonment.
   a. True*
   b. False

10. Institutional life teaches inmates to react to events without regard to the past or future.
    a. True*
    b. False

11. Inmate knives are usually intended for attacks on staff.
    a. True
    b. False*

12. Services ranging from sexual acts to special laundry procedures like starching shirts can be bartered on the black market of most prisons.
    a. True*
    b. False

13. The fact that cocaine is the most popular drug among inmates is best explained by imported factors.
    a. True
    b. False*

14. Each trade or sale in the hidden economy of the prison is part of a much larger network of relationships within and between cliques of prisoners.
    a. True*
    b. False

15. Coerced sex is probably more common than rape in most prisons.
    a. True*
    b. False

Essay and Discussion Items

1. What is prisonization and how does it affect inmates after release?

2. Contrast importation theory with deprivation theory. Which theory best explains prison life?

3. How does the prison economy operate and why do officials try to eliminate it?

4. What kinds of sexual activities are found in prisons?

5. How do prison authorities deal with contraband?

6. How are prison gangs organized and what role do they play in inmates' lives?

7. Into what types do most prisoner social roles fall? What behaviors and offenses are typical of each role?

8. Contrast the "causes" of prison riots to those of interpersonal violence among inmates.

Chapter Nine

Female Offenders

Learning Objectives

1. Describe the types of crime committed most often by females and explain how female crime rates have changed in the last twenty years.
2. Explain why women are often described as the "forgotten offenders."
3. Compare female inmate social organization and roles to those of males.
4. Identify the main areas in which female inmates receive differential treatment.
5. Discuss how women's programs should differ from those offered to men and explain the reasons for these differences.
6. Compare the health care problems faced by facilities for women with those holding men.
7. Discuss the special issues that are relatively unique to women's facilities.
8. Define a "co-correctional" facility and describe its advantages and liabilities for officials and inmates.

Chapter Outline

Introduction
The Crimes of Female Felons
Factors Affecting the Treatment of Women in the Justice System
Women as the "Forgotten Offenders"
Female Rates of Imprisonment
Female Inmate Social Organization
    Pseudo-Families
    The Social Roles of Female Inmates
    Discipline and Social Control in Women's Prisons
    Women's Adjustment to Prison Life
Programs for Women
    Health Care Issues
        Pregnant Inmates

HIV/AIDS Programs for Women
Older Women in Prison
Special Issues for Women's Prisons
Child Custody Issues
Sexual Harassment and Official Oppression
Co-Correctional Facilities
Summary

Major Points

1. Women are being imprisoned at a higher rate than ever before but the crimes they commit (e.g., theft, drugs) have changed little over the last thirty years.

2. Women are the "forgotten offenders" because there are relatively few of them, they cause less trouble than men, and they are not perceived as dangerous.

3. Women's social organization is usually an attempt to re-create the home and families they lost (or desired) before imprisonment.

4. Women are often disciplined for infractions that would be ignored in a men's facility and are more often sedated than men.

5. Women face many unique health care problems, not the least of which is the rapid growth of HIV-positive inmates. Pregnancy also presents a challenge to women's facilities.

6. The concept of parity is used to prevent gender discrimination in correctional facilities but sexual harassment remains a serious problem.

7. Child custody issues are much more important and common in women's facilities and may be used to increase the effectiveness of treatment.

8. Co-correctional facilities are often used to save money but they may benefit staff and male inmates more than women.

Key Terms

Co-correctional facility
(the) Cool
Economies of scale
(the) Life

Parity
Pseudo-families
Sexual harassment
(the) "Square"

Chapter Highlights

Although the percentage of females within prison populations has nearly doubled in recent years, the types of crimes committed by women remain predominantly drug and property offenses. Because they are relatively few in number and are rarely seen as dangerous by judges or the public, women are often called "forgotten offenders." Minor rules are more often enforced in female facilities and psychiatric labels are more often applied to women than to men. Women face more health care and child custody problems than do men. HIV-infection is increasing much faster among women than among men. Women's treatment should stress cooperation, assertiveness, and non-traditional jobs. Co-correctional facilities are often used to assure economies of scale for female prisons but may negatively impact female inmates.

Examination Questions

Multiple Choice Items

1. Women make up about _____ of those arrested.
   a. 5%
   b. 20%*
   c. 50%
   d. 75%

2. Women make up about _____ of prison inmates.
   a. 10%*
   b. 25%
   c. 40%
   d. 65%

3. Women are more often imprisoned for _____ than men.
   a. property crimes
   b. drug offenses
   c. prostitution
   d. all of the above*

4. Changes in sex roles have had _____ effect on the types of crimes committed by women.
   a. a major
   b. little or no*
   c. a controversial
   d. a minor

5. Female violations of _____ are treated more harshly than those of men.
   a. their traditional sex role.*
   b. traffic laws
   c. the civil type
   d. all of the above

6. Women are described as the "forgotten offenders" because they:
   a. contribute very little to prison populations.
   b. are not seen as particularly dangerous by sentencing judges, policy makers, or the public.
   c. are less violent than males while incarcerated.
   d. all of the above.*

7. The legal concept of _____ demands substantial equivalence, but not complete equality, between the treatment received by male and female inmates.
   a. discrimination
   b. parity*
   c. gender inequity
   d. due process

8. While men tend to recreate the violent city streets from which they came, it is the _____ that women try to recover in their informal convict society.
   a. courtship relationship
   b. sexual bonding
   c. traditional nuclear family*
   d. non-traditional vocational role

9. Convicted female offenders are _____ likely to be recidivists than men.
   a. more
   b. less*
   c. equally
   d. no studies have ever addressed this question

10. Which of the following is NOT true of the "pseudo-family" type of social organization?
    a. It is found in some facilities for female offenders.
    b. It is similar to a male gang.*
    c. It helps inmates deal with the loss of family ties.
    d. It helps inexperienced inmates adapt to prison life.

11. Females are described as "forgotten offenders" because:
    a. there are so few of them relative to males.
    b. they cause less trouble while imprisoned than men.
    c. they are considered less dangerous than males by the public.
    d. all of the above.*

12. The _____ is a relatively conventional woman with no allegiance to any criminal subculture who is comparable to the prosocial male.
    a. cool
    b. life
    c. square*
    d. hustler

13. A Texas study showed that women were charged with rule violations _____ men.
    a. more often than*
    b. less often than
    c. just as often as
    d. no such study has ever been published

14. Imprisoned women usually hold _____ views of sex roles.
    a. liberated
    b. polyglot
    c. traditional*
    d. widely varying

15. Imprisoned women are more impacted by loss of _____ than men.
    a. heterosexual relationships
    b. autonomy
    c. family contacts*
    d. mobility

16. Women's vocational programs should be designed to prepare them for:
    a. traditional female jobs.
    b. the roles of wife and mother.
    c. traditional male jobs.*
    d. the role of supervisor or executive.

17. Prisons could save millions in tax dollars just by providing female inmates with:
    a. health care programs that address women's needs.*
    b. offense-specific counseling.
    c. sex role training.
    d. mops and brooms.

18. The most effective treatment programs for women will stress:
    a. skills relevant to parenting.
    b. cooperative rather than competitive methods.
    c. group rather than individual efforts.
    d. all of the above.*

19. Training in _____ is especially needed by female inmates.
    a. housework
    b. assertiveness*
    c. cooperation
    d. building relationships

20. Pregnant inmates are most often found in:
    a. jails*
    b. prisons
    c. mortuaries
    d. all of the above

21. _____ states allow female inmates to stay with their newborn infants for more than a few hours.
    a. Two*
    b. Eight
    c. Twenty
    d. All

22. Women are _____ vulnerable to sexually transmitted diseases than males.
    a. more*
    b. less
    c. not
    d. no more

23. Research designed to help the mainstream society understand and deal with _____ has largely ignored the needs of women.
    a. HIV/AIDS*
    b. sex roles
    c. legal parity
    d. all of the above

24. One of the greatest traumas of imprisonment for many female inmates is the loss of:
    a. their husband or boyfriend
    b. their physical strength
    c. their educational opportunities
    d. their children*

25. The most pressing problem(s) faced by inmate-mothers include:
    a. being placed in facilities far from family members.
    b. lack of child-care and parenting programs.
    c. procedures that restrict the number, length, and quality of visits with children.
    d. lack of coordination between correctional agencies, child protective services, and foster care providers.
    e. all of the above.*

26. The rural location of most prisons affects women _____ than men.
    a. more negatively*
    b. more positively
    c. no less
    d. no more

27. Programs that try to unite inmate-mothers with their children are usually paid for by:
    a. the state department of correction.
    b. the federal government.
    c. welfare agencies.
    d. volunteers and charities.*

28. The privilege of being allowed to visit with one's children for women is similar to that of _____ for men.
    a. furlough
    b. conjugal visitation*
    c. early release
    d. life without parole

29. _____ exploitation of women is ancient and widespread in corrections.
    a. Sexual*
    b. Economic
    c. Legal
    d. All of the above

30. Many, but not all, states make it a _____ for anyone to use their official position as a government employee to coerce another to do as they desire.
    a. tort
    b. crime*
    c. policy violation
    d. requirement

31. When no action is taken on a sexual harassment complaint, the harassment often:
    a. disappears by itself.
    b. gets worse.*
    c. continues without change.
    d. any of the above.

32. The most effective way of reducing sexual harassment is to assure that women:
    a. hold a significant number of powerful positions within each agency.*
    b. are constantly armed with firearms.
    c. are trained in self-defense.
    d. are aware of the laws protecting them.

33. Correctional facilities that house both men and women are called:
    a. parity prisons.
    b. co-correctional institutions.*
    c. orgy sites.
    d. all of the above.

34. The sharing of prison space for male and female inmates is done mainly for _____ reasons.
    a. rehabilitative
    b. legal
    c. economic*
    d. social

35. Co-correctional facilities:
    a. achieve economies of scale that most women's prisons cannot achieve.
    b. allow more equality of access to programs to male and female prisoners.
    c. encourage men to behave less harshly towards one another and staff.
    d. all of the above.*

36. Of the co-correctional facilities now in operation, the most successful:
    a. have relatively equal numbers of men and women.
    b. house only non-violent prisoners with less than two years left in their sentence.
    c. have strict policies for transferring inmates to single-sex institutions as a penalty for improper behavior.
    d. all of the above.*

37. The fact that female inmates are more cooperative with staff and file fewer lawsuits than men contributes to:
    a. lack of public or official awareness of their problems.*
    b. the leniency with which they are treated.
    c. the massive deinstitutionalization of women in the 1990s.
    d. all of the above.

38. Which of the following is least important in understanding the actions of violent female offenders:
    a. the influence of a male associate.
    b. marijuana use.*
    c. a quarrel with a spouse or lover.
    d. domestic abuse.

True-False Items

1. It was not until the "progressives" of the late 1800s became concerned with women's prisons that their abuse and neglect by prison officials were even questioned.
    a. True*
    b. False

2. Women have not been affected by the current "get tough" approach to crime.
    a. True
    b. False*

3. Violent crimes by women are usually directed at strangers.
    a. True
    b. False*

4. Girls are more often arrested for minor status offenses like disobedience and running away than are boys.

a. True*
b. False

5. The variety of training, education, and rehabilitation programs in female prisons is greater than that found in male institutions.
   a. True
   b. False*

6. The legal concept of parity demands substantial equivalence, but not complete equality, between the treatment received by male and female inmates.
   a. True*
   b. False

7. The rarity of violence among women and their tendency to be cooperative have been used to justify the neglect of female prisoners.
   a. True*
   b. False

8. The "women's movement" has led to women adopting male norms that encourage a wider variety of crime than ever before among women.
   a. True
   b. False*

9. Women rarely commit acts of violence directed at strangers.
   a. True*
   b. False

10. Studies show that women's crime has not gotten more serious but that the whole system is now "tougher" on all offenses.
    a. True*
    b. False

11. Programs for women that reinforce sex role stereotypes make them vulnerable to domestic abuse, high-risk sexual behavior, and unwanted pregnancies.
    a. True*
    b. False

12. The sexual activity of women has always been much more regulated than that of men.
    a. True*
    b. False

13. In general, the lower the status of a woman relative to the men in power over her, the greater the likelihood of sexual harassment occurring.
    a. True*
    b. False

14. Women are abused in prison because they are more dangerous than male inmates.
    a. True
    b. False*

15. While men tend to recreate the violent city streets from which they came, it is the traditional nuclear family that women try to recover in their informal convict society.
    a. True*
    b. False

Essay and Discussion Items

1. How do the crimes of female felons differ from those of men? What trends appear to be affecting both genders equally?

2. Why are women called the "forgotten offenders?"

3. What forms of social organization are found in women's prisons? What unique needs do they meet?

4. Compare the prison social roles of men and women. How do they differ? How are they similar?

5. How are women affected by HIV? How should prison programs address these issues?

6. What child custody issues confront pregnant inmates and inmate-mothers? How can these best be used by treatment providers?

7. How does sexual harassment differ from discrimination? What behaviors are likely to be defined as sexual harassment?

8. What is a co-correctional facility and what advantages do they offer?

Chapter Ten

The Legal Rights of Offenders

Learning Objectives

1. Identify the reasons for allowing inmates and other offenders access to the courts.

2. List the main constitutional bases of prisoners' rights.

3. Describe how a felony conviction and imprisonment impact an individual's First Amendment rights.

4. Explain how the courts determine the privacy rights of prison inmates, staff, and visitors.

5. List and describe the areas to which the courts apply the Eighth Amendment ban on cruel and unusual punishment.

6. Discuss how the Fourteenth Amendment applies to prisoners and how it supplements other constitutional freedoms.

7. List the types of court actions filed by inmates and describe the goal of each type.

8. Describe how frivolous inmate lawsuits are controlled in the modern United States.

Chapter Outline

Introduction
Inmate Access to the Courts
First Amendment Rights
    Freedom of Religion
    Freedom of Speech
    Freedom of the Press
    Prisoner Mail
    Prisoner Unions and the Right to Assemble
Fourth Amendment Rights
    Searches of Parolees and Probationers
Eighth Amendment Rights

Major Points

1. Access to the courts is one of the most vital of all legal rights because it is essential to assuring virtually all other human rights.

2. Basic constitutional rights are severely restricted, but not entirely forfeited, as a result of a conviction and/or prison sentence.

3. First Amendment freedoms may be restricted for security or treatment needs as well as to protect other vital government interests.

4. Prison inmates, staff, and visitors have virtually no rights to privacy but search powers cannot be used to inflict punishment or unnecessarily embarrass a person.

5. The Fourteenth Amendment's guarantee of due process applies only when substantial liberty interests are at stake but all inmates in the same security category have a right to equal treatment unless reasonable suspicion justifies other treatment.

6. Most inmate legal actions are filed under section 1983 of the 1871 Civil Rights Act, but tort suits, habeas corpus petitions, and other types of legal processes are also seen.

7. Only the courts and the legislature may restrict inmates' ability to sue or otherwise seek redress of grievances through the judicial system.

8. A variety of methods are currently used to control inmate lawsuits and more are likely to be created by Congress.

Key Terms

Balancing test
Compensatory damages
Consent decree
Hands-off doctrine
Jailhouse lawyers
Legal mail
Liberty interest
Ombudsman
Prior restraint
Prison Litigation Reform Act
   of 1996

Procedural due process
Punitive damages
Qualified immunity
Rights-versus-privilege doctrine
Reasonable suspicion
Section 1983 of the Civil Rights Act
   of 1871
Special needs exception
Substantive due process
Tort
Writ of habeas corpus

Chapter Highlights

The "hands-off" era ended as the due process revolution encouraged the enforcement of rulings that permitted all persons access to the U.S. court system. Inmates have a few First Amendment rights but even these can be restricted if they interfere with pressing financial, security, or treatment needs. Staff and visitors give up most of their Fourth Amendment rights upon entering a correctional facility. Inmates may be searched whenever it is routine or if there is reasonable suspicion to single out one person for special treatment. The Eighth Amendment is applied to cases involving use of force, medical care, and the prison's obligation to protect inmates from one another and other foreseeable hazards. Due process is required only when a significant liberty interest is at stake but decisions may never be based solely on race, religion, or nationality. Most prison litigation uses Section 1983 of the Civil Rights act of 1871 but writs of habeas corpus and tort suits are also common. Only a judge or legislature can legally restrict inmate access to the courts but a variety of methods are available to judges to control frivolous lawsuits.

Examination Questions

Multiple Choice Items

1. The idea that it is illegal to deny inmates access to the courts was first recognized by the U.S. Supreme court in the:
   a. 1800s
   b. 1940s*
   c. 1960s
   d. 1980s

2. The most common basis for inmate lawsuits is:

   a. the Fourth Amendment to the U.S. Constitution.
   b. Section 1983 of the Civil Rights Act of 1871.*
   c. Section 3891 of the Civil Rights act of 1964.
   d. the Eighth Amendment to the U.S. Constitution.

3. Which of the following has the LEAST relevance to the legal rights of prison inmates?

   a. First Amendment.
   b. Fourth Amendment.
   c. Eighth Amendment.
   d. Tenth Amendment.*
   e. Fourteenth Amendment

4. Inmates were given access to the courts in:

   a. *ex parte Hull.**
   b. *Ruiz v. Estelle.*
   c. *Cooper v. Pate.*
   d. none of the above.

5. The 1971 case of _____ was the first time a court actually took control over the correctional conditions and practices of an entire state.

   a. *Ruiz v. Estelle*
   b. *ex parte Hull*
   c. *Holt v. Sarver**
   d. *Lewis v. Casey*

6. *Ruiz v. Estelle* is an important case because:

   a. it made the use of inmate-guards illegal.
   b. it declared severe overcrowding to be a violation of the Eighth Amendment.
   c. both of the above.*
   d. neither of the above.

7. Research shows that the operating expenses of most prisons were _____ by the *Ruiz* decision.

   a. drastically increased
   b. slightly decreased
   c. not significantly affected*
   d. greatly decreased

8. The tendency of the courts to refuse to hear legal challenges about prison conditions or administrative practices prior to the 1960s is known as the:

   a. hands-off doctrine.*
   b. Hull decision.
   c. habeas corpus doctrine.
   d. Eleventh Amendment.

9. A _____ allows an agency to correct a problem under the supervision of a court without admitting wrong-doing.
    a. consent decree*
    b. injunction
    c. judgement
    d. decision

10. A _____ is an official attempt to prevent the exercise of a freedom before it has been acted upon that is usually discouraged by the courts.
    a. prior restraint*
    b. habeas suit
    c. unilateral decree
    d. a priori law

11. A **habeas corpus** action is:
    a. a petition for the court to restore freedoms of speech or religion.
    b. a request for the Supreme Court to hear an appeal.
    c. a protest against cruel and unusual punishment.
    d. a challenge to the state's right to detain a person.*

12. Which of the following criteria are used by the courts to determine whether a religious group should have the right to practice its beliefs in a prison?
    a. the group's age.
    b. the group's similarity to other religions.
    c. the apparent sincerity of the believers.
    d. the costs that would result.
    e. all of the above.*

13. In _____ , the Supreme Court ruled that inmates with unconventional religious beliefs could not be subjected to discrimination and had all the rights possessed by prisoners of more popular faiths.
    a. *Cruz v. Beto**
    b. *Cooper v. Pate*
    c. *Holt v. Sarver*
    d. all of the above

14. A practice, omission, or act may not be protected by the First Amendment even if it is part of a legitimate religious belief system if it:
    a. threatens the security or discipline of the facility.
    b. interferes with the legal powers of institutional authorities.
    c. contradicts a reasonable facility rule.
    d. poses an excessive financial burden on the facility or jurisdiction.
    e. any of the above.*

15. Which of the following is protected by the First Amendment?
    a. threats, obscenity, and criminal conspiracies.
    b. statements that are likely to cause unnecessary panic, destruction, or danger.

    c. noisy speech at inappropriate times without good reason.

    d. verbal attacks on the government or its officials.*

    e. false statements that cause harm to others.

16. _____ statements are almost always protected by the First Amendment.

    a. Artistic

    b. Political*

    c. Incendiary

    d. All of the above

17. The most important result of the _____ ruling was the creation of a "reasonableness test" that guides officials and courts in deciding whether "legitimate penological interests" allow interference with Constitutional rights.

    a. *Mapp v. Ohio*

    b. *Turner v. Safley**

    c. *Procunier v. Martinez*

    d. *Harper v. Wallingford*

18. A prison rule is reasonable if:

    a. it had a valid connection with the government interests by which it was justified.

    b. there is an alternative method by which inmates can exercise the right in question.

    c. exercise of the right has significant effects on prison resources, staff, or inmates.

    d. there are no alternative methods to obtain the result desired by those who created it.

    e. any of the above are present.*

19. Only _____ mail is exempt from official censorship.

    a. private

    b. incoming

    c. legal*

    d. media

20. The reasonableness of a search is determined by the balance between security needs and privacy rights. This balance is judged on the basis of:

    a. the scope of the search.

    b. the place in which the search occurs.

    c. the manner in which the search is conducted.

    d. the reason for the search.

    e. all of the above.*

21. In suits over correctional searches, the courts:

    a. balance the need for the search against the loss of privacy that results from it.*

    b. require the searcher to obtain a warrant.

c. protect the rights of the powerless inmate.

d. observe the *nolo contendere* doctrine.

22. _____ consists of specific grounds that can be clearly articulated and lead an officer to believe criminal activity may be occurring.

a. Probable cause

b. Proof beyond a reasonable doubt

c. Reasonable suspicion*

d. Preponderance of evidence

e. Clear and convincing evidence

23. Prisoners are routinely searched when they:

a. enter a facility for the first time.

b. return from a furlough or outside work detail.

c. have had a contact visit with an outsider.

d. do any of the above.*

24. Searches of probationers and parolees require:

a. a warrant.

b. a state law permitting the practice.*

c. probable cause.

d. reasonable suspicion.

25. Under the Eighth Amendment, illegal conditions and practices are those that:

a. shock the conscience of the court and/or violate civilized standards of decency.

b. inflict unnecessary pain in a wanton manner.

c. are grossly disproportionate to the offender's crime.

d. indicate deliberate apathy to the basic human needs of the inmate.

e. do any of the above.*

26. Prisoners have the right to be protected from weather, staff abuses, other inmates, suicide, disease, and accidental injury under the _____ amendment.

a. 4th

b. 5th

c. 6th

d. 8th*

e. 14th

27. Constitutional rights are violated only when _____ on the part of staff leads to an injury.

a. negligence, callousness, or recklessness*

b. poor supervision or training

c. improper behavior

d. sloppiness or carelessness

28. A _____ is a civil wrong that results in injury or loss of money due to some-
    one else's failure to live up to his or her legal obligations.
    a. crime
    b. unconstitutional action
    c. tort*
    d. libel

29. _____ is required before a suit charging that medical care or other condi-
    tions violate the Eighth Amendment will be viewed as legitimate.
    a. "Inadequate attention"
    b. "Deliberate indifference"*
    c. A "violation of common sense"
    d. "Criminal neglect"

30. _____ must occur to apply the Eighth Amendment to the use of force by
    prison officials.
    a. "Unnecessary and wanton infliction of pain"*
    b. "Serious bodily injury"
    c. "Deliberate and life-threatening injury"
    d. "Psychological or physical pain and suffering"

31. The two critical clauses in the Fourteenth Amendment refer to:
    a. due process of law and equal treatment under law.*
    b. political speech and reasonable privacy.
    c. freedom of religion and protected statuses.
    d. all of the above.

32. A "liberty interest" is a right given to inmates by:
    a. a state law or policy.*
    b. the U.S. Constitution.
    c. the Declaration of Independence.
    d. the Federalist Papers.

33. Guidelines for disciplinary hearings were established by the Supreme Court
    in:
    a. *Wolff v. McDonnell.**
    b. *Hudson v. Macmillian.*
    c. *Wilson v. Seiter.*
    d. *Estelle v. Gamble.*

34. Prisoners have no right to _____ unless officially charged with a new
    crime.
    a. a trial by jury
    b. a court-appointed attorney*
    c. the right to confront and cross-examine informants
    d. any of the above

35. Psychiatric medication can be forced on an inmate if and only if:
    a. the inmate is dangerous to self or others.

b. taking the medication is in the best interests of the inmate.

c. the decision to force medication on the inmate is made in a hearing with the same due process protections as in serious disciplinary proceedings.

d. the decision is periodically reviewed by experts.

e. all of the above.*

36. ____means substantial, but not exact, equality in receiving access to privileges and treatment.

a. Equal treatment

b. Due process

c. Parity*

d. Status protection

37. Steps to control frivolous suits can be taken only by:

a. the prison warden or superintendent.

b. the legislature or the courts.*

c. the attorney general, president, or governor.

d. any of the above.

38. The Prison Litigation Reform Act of 1996 (PLRA) attempts to reduce the number of lawsuits filed in federal courts by prison inmates by:

a. forcing all inmates filing federal suits to pay a filing fee.

b. limiting how much can be awarded in attorney fees if the inmate wins.

c. prohibiting suits for psychological damages unless there is also physical injury.

d. allowing good time credits to be withdrawn for using the courts to harass officials.

e. all of the above.*

39. Only a ____ may forbid a specific inmate from filing further suits.

a. warden

b. judge*

c. governor

d. legislature

40. Inmate legal actions in federal courts may contest:

a. conditions of confinement.

b. the way in which a verdict was reached.

c. the manner in which a sentence was imposed.

d. any of the above.*

True-False Items

1. Convicted felons have less control over their privacy than do ordinary citizens but are entitled to certain liberties that protect their basic dignity as human beings.

a. True*

b. False

2. Every prison and jail in the U.S. is required to have either paralegals or a law library for inmate use.
   a. True
   b. False*

3. It is the "totality of conditions," rather than any one aspect of the prison, that is the central issue in Eighth Amendment cases.
   a. True*
   b. False

4. Prison inmates have a constitutional right to engage in any religious practice they choose and authorities are no longer able to restrict such activities until after criminal acts have occurred.
   a. True
   b. False*

5. Religious practices can be limited for financial or security reasons but beliefs may not be restricted.
   a. True*
   b. False

6. The First Amendment protects profits from published materials as well as speech and publication rights.
   a. True*
   b. False

7. Prisons and jails routinely examine all items mailed to and by inmates to assure that contraband or escape plans are not being transmitted.
   a. True*
   b. False

8. Only when a prisoner is singled out for special treatment is there a need to justify the search.
   a. True*
   b. False

9. Prisoners rarely have charges dismissed as a result of a hearing because the authorities have wide latitude in determining guilt.
   a. True*
   b. False

10. Inmates have very few rights beyond equal treatment and due process in disciplinary hearings.
    a. True*
    b. False

11. An inmate can be singled out for search at any time for any or no reason.
    a. True
    b. False*

12. The prison litigation reform act (PLRA) granted inmates many new rights and restricted the powers of prison officials to those areas that have been proven to affect security.
    a. True
    b. False*

13. The ability to restrict inmate lawsuits lies with the governor.
    a. True
    b. False*

14. Fewer than eight examples of legitimate inmate lawsuits filed since 1975 can be named.
    a. True
    b. False*

15. We are currently in the hands-off era of prisoners' rights, meaning that the legislature is forbidden from restricting prisoners' freedoms.
    a. True
    b. False*

Essay and Discussion Items

1. Why is inmate access to the courts such a vital right? Who controls this right under modern case law?

2. What religious speech and assembly rights are available to prison inmates? Under what circumstances can these be restricted?

3. What guidelines cover searches of inmates? What conditions must be present before parole/probation officers can search their clients' homes, cars, and persons?

4. What rights do inmates have under the Eighth Amendment's prohibition of "cruel and unusual punishment"? What is the most crucial case in defining these rights?

5. Describe the rights of an inmate facing a disciplinary hearing. Compare these rights to those of a trial.

6. Under what circumstances are inmates entitled to due process? How is the "Equal Protection under Law" clause of the Fourteenth Amendment applied in prison cases?

7. List the three most common types of legal actions filed by prison inmates. What does each seek and in what type of court is each filed?

8. How can a court respond if it determines an inmate's lawsuit to be frivolous? What actions has the U.S. Congress taken to control inmate lawsuits?

Chapter Eleven

Correctional Programs

Learning Objectives

1. Distinguish between "habilitative" and "rehabilitative" programs.

2. Describe the nature of the academic, vocational, religious, recreational, and life skills programs in penal institutions.

3. Explain the differences between basic treatment amenability and differential intervention strategies in addressing criminal behavior patterns.

4. Discuss the nature of cognitive therapy and list the reasons it is preferred in correctional settings.

5. Compare the twelve step approach with that used in other forms of group therapy.

6. Describe the methods used to address the unique problems of sex offenders and differentiate the frequency of their actual re-offense rate from that portrayed by the media.

7. Explain the sequence of events that leads to relapse, the importance of seemingly unimportant decisions in this cycle, and the strategies used to control relapse.

8. Explain why the types of programs that will have the most effect on offenders are rejected as unacceptable by the power structure of the prison.

Chapter Outline

Introduction
Habilitative Programs
  Academic Programs
    Literacy Programs
    GED Preparation
    College Classes
    The Value of Academic Programs
  Vocational Training
    Private Sector Involvement in Prison Industrial Training

Major Points

1. Habilitative programs such as literacy, GED, and life skills give offenders skills they failed to acquire during ordinary socialization.

2. Academic and vocational programs can prepare inmates for employment and promote the kind of self-esteem that inhibits criminal behavior.

3. Recreation functions mainly to keep inmates occupied but has the potential to benefit them in many ways if properly utilized.

4. Basic treatment amenability examines the ability of the individual to reform and assumes that all offenders will benefit from certain programs while differential intervention strategies address specific problems unique to subgroups of inmates.

5. Treatment may occur in individual psychotherapy, clinical groups, or twelve-step groups, the latter being over-used and the first being too expensive for frequent use.

6. Although psychoanalytic, humanist, and behavioral approaches have a place in corrections, most agencies now rely mainly on cognitive approaches that focus on the decision-making skills of the offender.

7. Compulsive behaviors like addiction require specialized treatment that gives special attention to relapse prevention.

8. The most effective programs empower offenders by teaching assertiveness and self-confidence but are usually rejected by prison power structures that believe maintaining the practical and moral superiority of staff over inmates is essential to facility operations.

Key Terms

Basic treatment amenability
Chemical castration
Civil commitment
Cognitive therapies
Differential intervention
Habilitative services
Learning disorders
Life skills

Literacy
Relapse prevention
Responsibility model
Seemingly unimportant decisions
  (SUDS)
Thinking errors
Twelve-step group

Chapter Highlights

Habilitative programs like literacy and life skills give offenders basic skills that most people acquire early in life. Vocational and academic programs prepare inmates for gainful employment. Partnerships between prisons and the private sector can be especially useful in promoting vocational training and basic work skills. Basic treatment amenability attempts to determine which offenders are most open to change and asserts that most have very similar problems regardless of the type(s) of offense(s) of which they have been convicted. Cognitive therapies, often using behavioral rewards, are at the core of most modern correctional programs because they reduce recidivism better than any other type. Clinical groups are also extremely cost-effective and thus popular in corrections. However, agencies tend to over-rely on twelve-step groups because they are free. Learning to deal with the stress, fantasies, and seemingly unimportant decisions that lead to relapse is crucial for offenders whose crimes are the result of compulsive behaviors. Unfortunately, most offenders need to develop assertiveness and self-confidence. These kinds of programs are perceived as threats to the moral superiority of staff and are thus rejected by most officials.

Examination Questions

Multiple Choice Items

1. Programs designed to help inmates acquire skills that most people learn through early socialization are referred to as:
   a. relapse prevention efforts.
   b. habilitative programs.*
   c. offense-specific treatment.
   d. psychoanalytic therapies.

2. Correctional programs may be found in:

   a. prisons.
   b. communities.
   c. jails.
   d. all of the above.*

3. Habilitative programs include _____ programs.

   a. academic
   b. vocational training
   c. life skills
   d. recreational
   e. all of the above*

4. The largest group of "treatment" providers in most prison systems is composed of:

   a. social workers
   b. case managers
   c. teachers*
   d. psychologists

5. A General Equivalency Diploma (GED) shows that a person has achieved:

   a. the skills required for a high school diploma.*
   b. the requirements of a college degree.
   c. basic literacy.
   d. vocational competence.

6. Inmates may take college classes:

   a. within a few prisons.
   b. by correspondence.
   c. by use of furloughs.
   d. by any of the above, although c. is rare.*

7. Which of the following best describes the attitude of most inmates toward treatment?

   a. They enjoy the programs and wish there were more of them.
   b. They avoid them because they require hard work and can be painful.*
   c. They enjoy them because they allow them to socialize with women.
   d. They distrust them because staff support for them is so strong.

8. Academic programs:

   a. provide the basis for the kind of self-esteem that inhibits crime.
   b. encourages self-discipline and a sense of investment in society.
   c. are correlated with lowered recidivism rates.
   d. all of the above.*

9. Which of the following is most appropriate and necessary for most inmates?

   a. college classes.
   b. hygiene training.

    c. vocational training.*

    d. team sports.

10. Prisons often define _____ as vocational training even though it accomplishes little of value for the inmate.

    a. unskilled, dull, and demeaning work assignments*

    b. literacy classes

    c. recreation

    d. religious services

11. Private companies are reluctant to use inmates because of:

    a. insurance problems.

    b. the need to train and motivate them.

    c. the violence, theft, and bureaucracy that are so much a part of prison life.

    d. all of the above.*

12. Vocational training should focus on:

    a. good work habits.

    b. specific job skills.

    c. both of the above.*

    d. neither of the above.

13. Which of the following is true of training and work programs in prisons?

    a. Administrators and voters see industries as a way to make money for the institution and reduce taxes.

    b. Work supervisors want to stress training and productivity.

    c. Inmates want to earn money.

    d. Staff want to keep inmates busy.

    e. All of the above.*

14. _____ is the oldest form of correctional treatment.

    a. Literacy education

    b. Vocational training

    c. Religious programming*

    d. Recreation

15. To have a "corrective" or therapeutic effect, discipline should do each of the following EXCEPT:

    a. constantly emphasize the individual's responsibility for all of their actions.

    b. have a minimum of rules that offenders understand to be in their best interests.

    c. use "natural consequences" or constructive tasks as penalties.

    d. use the most severe punishments allowed by law.*

    e. recognize and reward all client achievements.

16. _____ focuses on differences in each person's ability and willingness to cooperate with treatment providers rather than their type of crime, motive, or background.

    a. Differential intervention strategies

b. Basic treatment amenability*
c. Cognitive therapy
d. Habilitative programming

17. _____ claim that offenders must be classified according to the underlying causes of their criminality before experts can decide which programs can best address their behavior problems.
    a. Differential intervention strategies*
    b. Basic treatment amenability
    c. Cognitive therapy
    d. Habilitative programming

18. _____ therapies focus on the conscious thoughts and emotions of the offender in order to help her/him bring emotions under rational control, examine all methods of solving each problem that confronts them, and confront all varieties of thinking errors.
    a. Psychoanalytic
    b. Behaviorist
    c. Cognitive*
    d. Humanist

19. _____ have been shown to have better effects on recidivism than other types of treatment.
    a. Cognitive therapies*
    b. Self-esteem courses
    c. Recreational therapy
    d. Religious conversion

20. _____ therapies are most common for financial reasons.
    a. Individualized
    b. Group*
    c. Recreational
    d. Religious

21. The ideal clinical group would consist of _____ offenders and a professional therapist.
    a. 2 or 3
    b. 6 to 10*
    c. 20 to 30
    d. 40 or more

22. For a counseling group to be effective, each member must:
    a. feel worthwhile and accepted no matter what he or she says.
    b. keep focused on the specific goal of the session.
    c. take an active role in the group's work.
    d. acknowledge every other person in the group as a worthwhile equal.
    e. do all of the above.*

23. The most common types of groups in modern corrections are based on:
    a. cognitive principles.
    b. rational-emotive therapy.
    c. the twelve steps of Alcoholics Anonymous.*
    d. Freudian ideals.

24. Twelve-step groups:
    a. do not require the presence of a therapist.
    b. have been used with behaviors ranging from eating disorders to sex offenses.
    c. use stigma to promote self-esteem by focusing attention on the ability to control a problem behavior.
    d. are most effective with middle class, middle aged, white males.
    e. all of the above.*

25. Which of the following plays the largest role in twelve-step groups?
    a. religion.*
    b. cognitive principles.
    c. professional counselors.
    d. education about the problem behavior.

26. The most common forms of specialized treatment are for
    a. substance abusers.*
    b. sex offenders.
    c. anger control.
    d. stress management.

27. Prison administrators say that the most pressing need is for _____ treatment programs.
    a. substance abusers
    b. sex offenders*
    c. anger control
    d. stress management

28. Approximately _____ of the offenders who need drug treatment are thought to be receiving it at present.
    a. 5%
    b. 20%*
    c. 40%
    d. 80%

29. Counselors who deal with _____ must dictate which thoughts, feelings, and actions are proper and resist believing much of what clients tell them unless it is proven by some impartial method.
    a. violent offenders
    b. drug addicts
    c. sex offenders*
    d. property criminals

30. Compulsive offenders must be trained to recognize _____ if they are to break through their denial and avoid relapse.
    a. anger and depression
    b. all types of drugs
    c. seemingly unimportant decisions*
    d. the need for punishment

31. _____ are choices that place a person in situations that create opportunities for a relapse even though the action seems like reasonable and proper behavior.
    a. Cognitive errors
    b. Compulsive behaviors
    c. Seemingly unimportant decisions*
    d. All of the above

32. People with compulsive behavior problems often use fantasies to:
    a. create euphoria.
    b. deal with stress.*
    c. deny reality.
    d. all of the above.

33. Effective treatment:
    a. gives offenders power over their own lives.
    b. links offenders' self-respect to productive activities.
    c. allows assertive behavior toward staff.
    d. does all of the above.*

34. Prisons are designed to:
    a. destroy inmates' self-respect.
    b. assure that inmates remain dependent on staff.
    c. hold offenders with as little trouble or expense as possible.
    d. do all of the above.*

35. Despite its demonstrated effectiveness in reducing recidivism, "active" treatment is unpopular with officials because it:
    a. makes employee work routines more complicated.
    b. could attract public criticism for "leniency."
    c. questions the absolute moral superiority of staff over inmates.
    d. does all of the above.*

36. The demands of _____ contradict those of effective treatment and are at the root of many correctional failures.
    a. punishment*
    b. cost-cutting
    c. control
    d. all of the above

37. The major themes of an effective treatment program should include:
    a. making the client aware of the impact of the choices he/she makes in daily life.
    b. a refusal to allow the offender to consider him/herself a victim.
    c. recognizing and rewarding success in client behavior.
    d. maintaining the clinical focus on the central issue of offending behavior.
    e. all of the above.*

38. Most correctional treatment occurs while offenders are:
    a. on probation or parole.*
    b. not yet ready to change.
    c. in prison.
    d. awaiting trial.

39. The most effective treatment programs directly address the offender's:
    a. decision-making skills.*
    b. self-conscious conflicts.
    c. early childhood traumas.
    d. recreational opportunities.

40. Which of the following is true of correctional treatment?
    a. Vocational training is the most pressing need in modern prisons.
    b. Cognitive-behavioral techniques are at the core of most current programs.
    c. Educational programs have been shown to reduce recidivism but are becoming rare.
    d. Most treatment occurs while offenders are on probation or parole.
    e. All of the above.*

True-False Items

1. Habilitative services teach skills that are basic to life; they are needed because of a failure in the original socialization process rather than a subsequent loss of skills.
    a. True*
    b. False

2. The current belief among most criminologists is that thoughts and behavior are at the root of criminality while self-esteem is only a symptom of the problem(s).
    a. True*
    b. False

3. Prison inmates receive almost one out of every four dollars awarded by the government for college tuition in Pell grants every year.
    a. True
    b. False*

4. Virtually all types of prison treatment programs reduce recidivism if they are properly designed and operated.
   a. True*
   b. False

5. Basic treatment amenability is often called a "one-size-fits-all" approach by critics.
   a. True*
   b. False

6. Cognitive therapy focuses on the offender's past experiences, especially those in early childhood.
   a. True
   b. False*

7. Individual counseling is the most commonly offered type of treatment in most prisons.
   a. True
   b. False*

8. The text infers that twelve-step groups are over-used in corrections because they are cheap.
   a. True*
   b. False

9. Most sex offenders cannot be effectively treated and will reoffend if released, whether or not they are supervised.
   a. True
   b. False*

10. Many addicts and sex offenders suffer from compulsive disorders that result in crime.
    a. True*
    b. False

11. Even the thought of their compulsive behavior is pleasing to an addict or sex offender.
    a. True
    b. False*

12. If effective types of treatment are used, relapse should be of little concern in corrections.
    a. True
    b. False*

13. Stress often leads to fantasies of criminal acts which, in turn, can lead to relapse.
    a. True*
    b. False

14. Treatments that encourage inmates to be assertive and self-confident are popular among modern prison officials.
    a. True*
    b. False

15. The most effective treatments encourage inmates to be assertive and self-confident but are usually rejected by prison officials.
    a. True*
    b. False

Essay and Discussion Items

1. What are "habilitative programs?"
2. How does "basic treatment amenability" differ from "differential intervention strategies?" Must officials always choose one of these approaches?
3. What obstacles discourage the private sector from assisting in the vocational training of inmates?
4. What is "cognitive therapy?"
5. How do clinical and twelve-step groups differ?
6. What kinds of treatment are most needed and desired by correctional administrators?
7. How do correctional administrators feel about treatment? Why?
8. Why are prisons actually poor places for effective treatment to occur?

Chapter Twelve

Managing the Prison

Learning Objectives

1. Describe the areas covered by prison rules, the importance of various types of rules, and the methods by which rules are enforced.
2. Define "contraband" and explain how and why authorities try to control it.
3. Explain why and how it is necessary for guards and inmates to collaborate in the routine life of the prison.
4. Describe how stress and burnout affect correctional practitioners and how their impact can be minimized.
5. Describe the impact of changes in the racial and gender makeup of prison staffs.
6. Define a bureaucracy and relate its basic traits to the advantages and liabilities of this form of organization.
7. Define the three basic types of power and discuss how they are used by correctional authorities.
8. Explain why private prisons have become popular in recent years and list the problems they pose for society.

Chapter Outline

Introduction
Prison Security
    Prison Rules and Their Enforcement
    Preventing Escapes
    Controlling Contraband
    Prison Rule Violators
    Inmate-Guard Collaboration
Custodial Staff Responsibilities
    Stress and Burnout among Correctional Practitioners
    Job Satisfaction among Correctional Staff
    Female Correctional Officers

Major Points

1. Security is the main concern of any prison and rules designed to prevent escapes, control contraband, and assure order cover most aspects of inmate life.

2. Correctional officers perform a variety of roles within the prison and many must obtain the tacit cooperation of inmates if they are to adequately perform their jobs.

3. Female COs have concerns that are typical of women in other traditionally "blue-collar" fields, but racial tensions among prison staff often parallel those of the convict culture.

4. As professionalism and diversity increase, job satisfaction often declines in corrections and other fields and burnout is a problem for all who work with troubled populations.

5. Correctional agencies are very bureaucratic and centralization of authority is a new trend facilitated by technology and the desire to cut government budgets that frustrates many corrections professionals.

6. Correctional agencies have long used coercive methods to manage both staff and offenders but some agencies are turning to more participative styles of administration as their staff professionalizes and the benefits of unit management are realized.

7. Privatization is a popular trend designed to cut costs and increase efficiency, while protecting the government from lawsuits.

8. The ability of the private sector to cut costs and put public interests ahead of stockholder profits is still under vigorous debate.

Key Terms

Administrative convenience
Authoritative management
Bureaucracy
Burnout
Chain of command
Coercive power
Contraband
Correctional officers
The "count"
Cross-train

Normative power participative
   management
Profession
Remunerative power
"Shakedown"
Span of control
Unit management
Unity of command
The yard

Chapter Highlights

Prisons assure custody and control through the enforcement of rules that control most inmate activities. Minor "nuisance" violations are often tolerated to assure inmate cooperation with staff but serious rule violations that might lead to escapes, smuggling of contraband, or violence are rarely ignored. Correctional officers work directly with inmates in cell blocks, shops, classrooms, and the "yard.". Others stand guard in wall posts or have administrative duties. Job assignments may stress bureaucratic and/or "people" skills but are usually made on the basis of administrative convenience. Stress and burnout are common among professionals who work with people who have problems but are especially troublesome for prison staff. Women and minorities are increasingly common in the prison workforce and have brought many innovations to corrections but still encounter prejudice and discrimination. Correctional agencies are extremely bureaucratic and some use coercive methods to control staff as well as inmates. Modern administrators, however, are coming to recognize that participative strategies like unit management are most productive with professional workforces. The impact of privatization on cost-efficiency is still being assessed; many actual and potential problems have been noted in the growing but concentrated industry.

Examination Questions

Multiple Choice Items

1. Which of the following is of LEAST concern to prison authorities?
    a. Assuring custody of inmates
    b. Rehabilitating inmates*
    c. Keeping inmates under control
    d. Controlling costs

2. Crowding can increase prison costs by:
    a. making more work for staff.
    b. threatening security.
    c. increasing wear on the physical facility.
    d. all of the above.*

3. Correctional officials avoid the media because of:
    a. security concerns.
    b. lack of time.
    c. staff shortages.
    d. media focus on unusual events.
    e. all of the above.*

4. Correctional officers are best described as the _____ of the prison.
    a. police force*
    b. treatment staff
    c. administrative elite
    d. all of the above

5. Prison rules:
    a. restate laws.
    b. reinforce mainstream norms.
    c. grow in number as unusual events occur.
    d. all of the above.*

6. It costs an average of _____ to deal with a single major rule violation.
    a. $75
    b. $550
    c. $970*
    d. $2020

7. Escapes are _____ in modern prisons.
    a. extremely common
    b. quite rare*
    c. of little concern
    d. all of the above

8. The most common method of keeping track of inmates is the:
    a. lockdown.
    b. count.*
    c. shakedown.
    d. electronic monitor.

9. In a prison, _____ is any item that inmates are not explicitly allowed to possess.
    a. pruno
    b. contraband*
    c. barter
    d. hooch

10. Inmates use _____ as weapons.
    a. crude knives called "shivs"
    b. boiling water
    c. lighter fluid
    d. all of the above*

11. Official records show that known rule violators are often each of the following EXCEPT:
    a. older, more experienced prisoners.*
    b. African-American.
    c. inmates with many prior convictions.
    d. male.

12. _____ are usually among the most well-behaved prisoners and are at very low risk of recidivism.
    a. Drug offenders
    b. Murderers*
    c. Violent offenders
    d. Muggers

13. Guards may be corrupted by:
    a. extortion.
    b. blackmail.
    c. bribery.
    d. all of the above.*

14. Correctional officers who are fearful of inmates tend to be:
    a. lenient in enforcing rules.
    b. punitive towards inmates.*
    c. easily corrupted.
    d. all of the above.

15. Guard attitudes towards inmates are predicted by:
    a. the facility's security level.
    b. the traits of the inmate they deal with.
    c. the particular job assignment they hold.
    d. all of the above.*

16. Which of the following job assignments would NOT place a CO in direct contact with inmates?
    a. cell block
    b. wall post*
    c. yard
    d. shop or school

17. The _____ is/are described as one of the least structured and most dangerous areas of the prison.
    a. cell block
    b. yard*

    c. shop or industrial area

    d. agricultural fields

18. COs are usually assigned to specific jobs on the basis of:

    a. civil service exams.

    b. seniority.

    c. administrative convenience.*

    d. the spoils system.

19. Most definitions of a profession emphasize:

    a. special training or credentials.

    b. a distinct mission.

    c. adherence to an code of ethics.

    d. self-regulation of members' conduct.

    e. all of the above*

20. _____ is a state of emotional exhaustion in which the person feels they have accomplished little at their job that is common among people in the "helping professions."

    a. Burnout*

    b. Stress

    c. Overload

    d. All of the above

21. Correctional careers are unattractive to many people because of:

    a. the remote locations of most prisons.

    b. low wages.

    c. lack of public respect.

    d. all of the above.*

22. Approximately _____ % of prison guards are women.

    a. 5

    b. 25*

    c. 40

    d. 65

23. Covert discrimination against female guards most often takes the form of :

    a. sexually-oriented jokes and comments.

    b. practical jokes and pranks.

    c. poor job evaluations by superiors.*

    d. all of the above.

24. Women are often visible as prison guards and _____ but are rarely found in supervisory positions.

    a. administrators*

    b. spokespersons

    c. kitchen attendants

    d. legislators

25. Because they do not socialize together, _____ staff often develop false beliefs about each other which in turn continue their cliquishness and belief in stereotypes.
    a. male and female
    b. traditional and modern
    c. white and black*
    d. all of the above

26. Prison staff are managed according to a combination of principles drawn mainly from:
    a. the military and bureaucracy.*
    b. democracy.
    c. utilitarian totalitarianism.
    d. science and education.

27. _____ describes the flow of commands from administrators to managers, supervisors and employees, and the flow of information from staff to administrators.
    a. Span of control
    b. Chain of command*
    c. Unity of command
    d. None of the above

28. The specific number of people who report directly to a supervisor or administrator is known as:
    a. span of control.*
    b. chain of command.
    c. unity of command.
    d. none of the above.

29. _____ creates a situation in which each employee has one, and only one, supervisor.
    a. Span of control
    b. Chain of command
    c. Unity of command*
    d. None of the above

30. Which of the following is **not** typical of a bureaucracy?
    a. hierarchial organization of authority
    b. specialized division of labor
    c. use of rules to guide all decision-making
    d. consistent focus on the needs of those being served*
    e. seeing one's job as a career

31. Advantages of bureaucratic organization include:
    a. standard methods of handling cases that minimize discretionary judgements.
    b. easy and quick replacement of employees.

c. efficient handling of a large number of cases by a small number of staff.

d. all of the above.*

32. The formal organization of the prison uses _____ power as the primary method for controlling inmates and _____ power as the primary method of controlling employees.

    a. remunerative/normative*
    b. coercive/remunerative
    c. normative/coercive
    d. coercive/normative

33. Which of the following areas would include medical and dental services?

    a. custody
    b. programs*
    c. management
    d. industry/agriculture

34. _____ power is the most effective in creating loyalty and encouraging cooperation.

    a. Remunerative
    b. Coercive
    c. Democratic
    d. Normative*

35. Most correctional agencies use _____ style of management that stresses the rank and power of each employee.

    a. a participative
    b. a professional
    c. a seniority
    d. an authoritative*

36. _____ management encourages employees to invest in all of the agency's operations and decisions by encouraging them to suggest ways to improve their own performance and that of the agency.

    a. Participative*
    b. Militaristic
    c. Remunerative
    d. Punitive

37. Approximately _____ % of U.S. inmates are held in privately operated facilities.

    a. 3*
    b. 12
    c. 35
    d. 52

38. Corrections Corporation of America and Wackenhut Corrections Corporation now control _____ of all the privately managed prison beds in the world.
    a. about one out of four
    b. nearly half
    c. over three-fourths*
    d. virtually all

39. Which of the following is LEAST likely to be operated by a private company?
    a. a minimum security facility
    b. a maximum security facility*
    c. a juvenile facility
    d. a county jail

40. Possible advantages of private prisons include:
    a. reduced construction and operating costs.
    b. less government liability in lawsuits.
    c. better designed and more modern facilities.
    d. more focus on employee performance rather than seniority.
    e. all of the above.*

True-False Items

1. All the social problems of a large city can be found, often in concentrated form, within a prison.
   a. True*
   b. False

2. The media are usually well informed on correctional topics and base most stories on numerous visits and extensive interviews.
   a. True
   b. False*

3. Prisons regulate nearly every aspect of life to assure security, cut costs, and reduce the workload of administrators and staff.
   a. True*
   b. False

4. COs will sometimes ignore minor violations involving nuisance items, but only the most corrupt will overlook serious contraband.
   a. True*
   b. False

5. Like crime in general, most rule violations are minor and go unnoticed and unreported.
   a. True*
   b. False

6. There is no evidence that racial or gender discrimination affects the manner in which prison rules are enforced.
   a. True*
   b. False

7. Prisons must try to preserve the dignity of inmates while avoiding practices that discriminate on the basis of gender in evaluating and promoting staff.
   a. True*
   b. False

8. Prison staff are managed according to a combination of principles drawn from the military and bureaucracy.
   a. True*
   b. False

9. Because they are politically controlled, correctional bureaucracies are very sensitive to the desires of the people they serve.
   a. True
   b. False*

10. Professional bureaucrats are trusted to use their personal judgement to decide how cases should be handled.
    a. True
    b. False*

11. Correctional staff focus on the criminal acts and legal status of the person which is alienating to both the practitioner and the client but helps them protect the public.
    a. True*
    b. False

12. The more power a person or agency possesses, the less responsibility they have for their actions.
    a. True
    b. False*

13. Prisons are notorious for being coercive towards employees as well as inmates even though organizational efficiency studies uniformly condemn this approach.
    a. True*
    b. False

14. Private sector corrections has become a very concentrated industry with two companies controlling 75% of the inmates in corporate custody.
    a. True*
    b. False

15. Studies clearly show that private prisons are cheaper, more effective in reducing recidivism, and more skilled at handling staff than those operated by the government.
    a. True
    b. False*

Essay and Discussion Items

1. What are the main goals of prison security? What activities do they cover and how well are they enforced?

2. What kinds of job assignments are given to correctional officers? What skills are required of each?

3. What is a "profession"? Which correctional practitioners are professionals?

4. What kind of relationship do most correctional agencies have with the media? Why?

5. What is burnout, why does it occur, and what can be done to offset its effects?

6. Compare the problems encountered by women and minorities when they enter the prison workforce? How might each best be addressed?

7. Compare bureaucratic norms with professional ones. What type of management is best suited to each?

8. What are the advantages of private prisons? What ethical, practical, and political problems do they pose?

Chapter Thirteen

The Death Penalty

Learning Objectives

1. Describe the history of capital punishment in Western society and its effect on modern use of execution in the U.S.
2. Explain the changes in imposing the death penalty that resulted from the *Furman* and *Gregg* decisions.
3. Describe how the recent imposition of limits on appeals of capital sentences will affect the rate and costs of executions in the U.S.
4. Outline the legal and moral issues involved when retarded, insane, or youthful persons are charged with a capital offense.
5. Identify geographic patterns in the use of execution in the modern U.S. and the problems in assuring that executions will be as humane as possible.
6. Compare the distribution of death row populations with those of actual executions in the post-Furman era and outline the problems faced by these inmates.
7. List the arguments most often used to support the use of capital punishment and discuss the validity of each.
8. List the arguments most often used by opponents of capital punishment and discuss the validity of each.

Chapter Outline

Introduction
The History of Capital Punishment
Modern Criteria for Use of the Death Penalty
    Legal Processes in Capital Trials
    Limiting Appeals of Death Sentences
    The Costs of Capital Punishment
Special Groups and the Use of Capital Punishment
    The Insane
    The Mentally Retarded

Major Points

1. The death penalty has traditionally been used to punish those acts felt to threaten the power structure of society and has often been disproportionately used against disenfranchised populations.

2. The death penalty can be applied only if specific aggravating factors described in the law are found to outweigh mitigating ones in a two-stage or bifurcated trial where guilt and punishment are handled separately.

3. Many people believe that it is far more expensive to imprison a person for life than to execute them; recent attempts to limit appeals of death sentences are unlikely to change this although they will probably increase the rate of executions in the U.S.

4. The insane cannot be executed but the retarded have no special protection; each state is free to decide the minimum age at which a person becomes eligible for execution.

5. Most states now use lethal injection to execute prisoners but the electric chair, gas chamber, and gallows are also permitted as are firing squads.

6. Most executions occur in the south, especially in Texas, but California, Illinois, and Pennsylvania have large death row populations.

7. Few criminologists believe that the death penalty has any deterrent effect, but the retributive and boundary-setting powers of capital punishment are significant.

8. Opponents of the death penalty feel that it is a national embarrassment and provide evidence that its brutalization effects may actually increase the murder rate.

Key Terms

Aggravating factors
Bifurcated trial process
Brutalization thesis
Capital punishment

Culpability
Mitigating factors
Opportunity cost
Writ of habeas corpus

Chapter Highlights

One of the oldest criminal punishments in human society, the death penalty has long been used to denote the acts felt to be most dangerous to society. The U.S. is one of the few industrialized democracies that still uses this sanction. As a result of the *Furman* and *Gregg* decisions, capital trials require a close examination of aggravating and mitigating factors specified in the penal code before a death sentence can be imposed. Recent limits of appeals will speed the rate of execution and many hope it will reduce the costs of executions which are now about three times those of life-without-parole. Most modern U.S. executions occur in the South, especially Texas, Virginia, and Florida. Lethal injection is the most common method of killing. Under current case law the insane cannot be executed but the retarded have no special protection and each state sets its own minimum age. Most criminologists and police chiefs reject the idea that executions deter crime but the retributive, incapacitative, and boundary-setting functions of capital punishment are undeniable. Opponents of the death penalty claim that it may inspire violent crimes and are embarrassed that a supposedly progressive nation uses such a punishment.

Examination Questions

Multiple Choice Items

1. The most liberal use of the death penalty in early America focused primarily on the need to control:
   a. slaves.*
   b. revolutionaries.
   c. rapists.
   d. outlaws.

2. _____ was the first state to abolish the death penalty.
   a. Texas
   b. Michigan*
   c. Maine
   d. Alabama

3. Executions became private affairs as a result of:
   a. court rulings that allowed "death with dignity" to the condemned.
   b. fear of the spectators' "animal instincts."*
   c. fear of lawsuits.
   d. public opinion.

4. All but a few of those executed in the U.S. for crimes other than murder were:
   a. traitors.
   b. racial minorities.*
   c. women.
   d. later proved innocent.

5. The death penalty was first used to deter certain drug offenses in the:
   a. 1800s.
   b. 1920s.
   c. 1950s.*
   d. 1980s.

6. The 1972 case of _____ declared all U.S. death penalty laws to be unconstitutional because they imposed capital punishment in an "arbitrary and capricious manner" that was often racially discriminatory.
   a. *Furman v. Georgia**
   b. *Woodson v. North Carolina*
   c. *Gregg v. Georgia*
   d. *Mapp v. Ohio*

7. In *Gregg v. Georgia*, the Supreme Court ruled that the death penalty was:
   a. unconstitutional.
   b. legal if imposed in a consistent and fair manner.*
   c. discriminatory in the way it was being used.
   d. none of the above.

8. A _____ trial process has two parts: the first decides guilt or innocence; the second part sets punishment by examining the aggravating or mitigating factors.
   a. bifurcated*
   b. bench
   c. negotiated
   d. grand jury

9. Due to new laws and procedures recently adopted by the Supreme Court, executions will become:
   a. quicker and more frequent.*

   b. slower and less frequent.

   c. more arbitrary.

   d. all of the above.

10. It is approximately _____ times more expensive to bring a capital case to trial as it is to bring a non-capital case to trial.

   a. two

   b. three*

   c. four

   d. no difference in trial costs

11. Opponents of capital punishment argue that its expense represents a huge _____ because money spent on the death penalty would be better used on other crime control strategies.

   a. brutality tariff

   b. deficit expenditure

   c. opportunity cost*

   d. deterrent cost

12. Which of the following groups or categories of people are **protected as a class** from being executed?

   a. those who commit crimes as juveniles

   b. the retarded

   c. the insane*

   d. all of the above are protected classes

13. Fifteen-year-olds can be executed only if:

   a. a judge and jury agree that the death penalty is appropriate.

   b. the state has a law permitting such use of capital punishment.*

   c. there is a complete lack of mitigating factors.

   d. all of the above are present.

14. The Supreme Court ruled it illegal to execute an insane person in:

   a. *Ford v. Wainwright* (1985).*

   b. *Furman v. Georgia* (1972).

   c. *McCleskey v. Zant* (1991).

   d. *Habeas v. Corpus* (1919).

15. Which of the following nations has NOT recently executed anyone for crime(s) committed as a juvenile?

   a. United States

   b. Russia*

   c. Yemen

   d. Iran

   e. Saudi Arabia

16. Which of the following is the MOST common method of execution used in the U.S. today?

   a. lethal injection*

b. electrocution

c. the gas chamber

d. hanging

e. firing squad

17. In recent history, botched executions have resulted from each of the following EXCEPT:

a. violent reactions to the mixture of drugs used in lethal injections.

b. serious problems in finding a vein that will hold the needle for lethal injection.

c. electric chair malfunctions.

d. poor aim by firing squads.*

18. The largest number of executions in the U.S. since *Gregg* have occurred in:

a. Florida.

b. Georgia.

c. New York.

d. Texas.*

19. Execution is clearly more popular in the _____ states than elsewhere in the nation.

a. Northern

b. Midwestern

c. Southern*

d. Western

20. Those who want to keep the death penalty are known as:

a. "Retentionists."*

b. "Conservatives."

c. "Abolitionists."

d. "Liberals."

21. Isaac Erlich's finding that executions had a deterrent effect are discounted by most criminologists because:

a. changes in morality and the distribution of wealth explain these findings.

b. Erlich assumed that an execution in Florida might deter a killing in Alaska.

c. both of the above.*

d. neither of the above; Erlich's findings are widely accepted in criminology.

22. The work of both Layson and Cameron supports a view of deterrence that has been popular among social scientists for many years. This belief maintains that the:

a. certainty of punishment is more powerful than severity.*

b. severity of punishment is more powerful than certainty.

c. certainty, severity, and swiftness are equally important in determining deterrent value.

d. capital punishment is the best available deterrent to murder ever identified.

23. The evidence suggests that making executions public again would _____ their deterrent effects.
    a. increase
    b. decrease*
    c. have no impact on
    d. no studies have examined this question

24. Retentionists believe that the death penalty is morally justified as a way of:
    a. assuring some victims' survivors a sense of justice.
    b. fulfilling society's obligation to assure justice.
    c. providing an important symbol of social boundaries and beliefs.
    d. all of the above.*

25. According to its supporters, the death penalty provides the public with:
    a. information about new social priorities.
    b. a sense of unity.
    c. both of the above.*
    d. neither of the above.

26. Moral arguments against the death penalty emphasize that:
    a. it lowers society to the level of the criminals it despises.
    b. it is a step away from the values that cherish individual lives.
    c. there is potential for executing innocent people.
    d. all of the above.*

27. Utilitarian arguments against capital punishment consist of:
    a. attacks on the penalty's deterrent effect.
    b. fears that executions may actually inspire people to kill others.
    c. the costs of the death penalty.
    d. all of the above.*

28. Executions may encourage more killings by:
    a. people seeking to become famous.
    b. people wishing to die at the hands of the government.
    c. creating a brutalization effect.
    d. any of the above.*

29. The brutalization thesis maintains that capital punishment may actually encourage criminal violence by encouraging potential killers to:
    a. identify with the state or the executioner.
    b. providing some citizens with a justification for killing those who offend them.
    c. exposing people to violence.
    d. all of the above.*

30. The majority of current death row inmates are:
    a. white.*
    b. African-American.

    c. Asian.
    d. Hispanic.

31. Studies show that there is _____ racial bias when defendants receive the death penalty if the nature of the crime is taken into account.
    a. only slight
    b. a lot of
    c. no*
    d. an unknown level of

32. Some people feel that the death penalty is used in a discriminatory manner in the post-Furman era because:
    a. very few whites have been executed.
    b. the killers of non-whites are rarely executed.*
    c. both of the above.
    d. neither of the above; there is general agreement that post-Furman statutes have made the death penalty non-biased.

33. In _____ the Supreme Court ruled that the tendency to execute the killers of whites more often than others did not violate the *Gregg* ruling.
    a. *Coker v. Jones* (1977)
    b. *Woodson v. North Carolina* (1976)
    c. *McCleskey v. Zant* (1991)*
    d. *Godfrey v. Georgia* (1980)

34. _____ is expected to result in more and quicker executions.
    a. The *McCleskey v. Zant* ruling
    b. The *Anti-terrorism and Effective Death Penalty Act of 1996 (ADEPA)**
    c. The *Ford v. Wainwright* ruling
    d. None of the above

35. _____ is the executive power to reduce a sentence and is a form of executive clemency that also includes the power to grant pardons.
    a. Commutation of sentence*
    b. Expiative recourse
    c. Gubernatorial discharge
    d. Appellate reversal

36. Arguments that claim the _____ of the death penalty is too high maintain that the money would be more effectively spent on other forms of crime control and prevention.
    a. opportunity cost*
    b. clemency potential
    c. monetary alternates
    d. all of the above

37. New legislation empowers the _____ to assure that use of federal death statutes are not racially biased.
    a. local U.S. attorney

b. U.S. Attorney General*
c. federal district courts
d. state appellate courts

38. Which of the following is a fact used by abolitionists to support their belief that use of capital punishment is still arbitrary?
    a. Only 1 to 2 percent of those eligible for the death penalty actually receive it.
    b. The first defendant to deal with the prosecutor is less likely than his or her partner to get the penalty regardless of their roles in the crime.
    c. There is great variation across regions, states, and jurisdictions as to how often the penalty is sought and obtained.
    d. All of the above are facts that support the view that the death penalty is imposed arbitrarily in the U.S.*

39. Surveys show that _____ of police chiefs in the U.S. believe that the death penalty is an effective deterrent to violent crime.
    a. 1%*
    b. 20%
    c. 55%
    d. 85%

40. Which of the following does NOT appear to be significant in determining a nation's views on capital punishment?
    a. religion
    b. politics
    c. efficiency*
    d. culture

True-False Items

1. The same data is often interpreted differently by those who abolish the penalty and those who would retain it.
   a. True*
   b. False

2. Throughout recorded history, death has been used to punish only murderers and soldiers.
   a. True*
   b. False

3. The *Anti-terrorism and Effective Death Penalty Act of 1996 (ADEPA)* gives persons sentenced to death one year to assemble and file their federal appeals.
   a. True*
   b. False

4. The United States is in violation of the *International Covenant on Civil and Political Rights* because it allows the execution of people for crimes committed as juveniles.
   a. True*
   b. False

5. Use of lethal injection has eliminated the potential for "botched" executions.
   a. True
   b. False*

6. Deterrence advocates believe that capital punishment is justified by the mere possibility that some innocent victim might be saved by it.
   a. True*
   b. False

7. Most criminologists believe that the death penalty has a significant deterrent effect.
   a. True
   b. False*

8. Studies of the "Furman commutees" show that these men were far more dangerous to prison staff and inmates than other killers and were more likely to be recidivists when released than any other group of violent offenders.
   a. True
   b. False*

9. At the base of the moral arguments against capital punishment is the belief that the more civilized a society becomes, the less it relies on violence to accomplish its goals.
   a. True
   b. False*

10. Executions may actually prolong the suffering of victims' families by repeatedly dragging details of the case through the media.
    a. True*
    b. False

11. Empirical support for the brutalization thesis is much stronger than that for deterrence.
    a. True
    b. False*

12. In the case of *Furman v. Georgia*, the Supreme Court used scientific data demonstrating racial discrimination to support its ruling.
    a. True*
    b. False

13. Many nations will not extradite drug lords and other fugitives to the U.S. if they might face the death penalty.
    a. True*
    b. False

14. Most police chiefs believe that the death penalty deters violent crimes.
    a. True
    b. False*

15. Most U.S. citizens prefer the death penalty to life-without-parole.
    a. True
    b. False*

Essay and Discussion Items

1. What forces have predicted the popularity of the death penalty in western history? What crimes were punished with death in the ancient, medieval, and industrial eras?

2. Describe the Supreme Court rulings that have shaped modern use of capital punishment in the U.S. What guidelines control its current use?

3. Under what circumstances can the death penalty be applied to retarded persons? What about the insane? Persons who committed offenses prior to their eighteenth birthday?

4. Where have most post-Furman executions occurred in the U.S.? Which states have the largest death row populations?

5. How do other western nations view capital punishment? What is the effect of our use of the death penalty on our international status?

6. Do scientific studies provide a firm basis for claims that capital punishment has a deterrent effect? Do they support the brutalization thesis?

7. Is it cheaper to execute people or confine them for life? What is assumed by those who argue for the cost-efficiency and retributive value of capital punishment? Do the facts support these claims?

8. What are the main arguments against capital punishment? What do these arguments presume about the nature of human behavior, society, and civilization? Are these assumptions valid?

Chapter Fourteen

The Future of Corrections

Learning Objectives

1. Describe how media images of the "crime problem" affect the correctional mission.
2. Explain how the "war on drugs" will effect the size and traits of the U.S. prison population.
3. Identify the reasons for rising rates of imprisonment.
4. List the direct and indirect costs of rising imprisonment rates.
5. Describe how the victims' movement has affected the nature and duties of the correctional system.
6. List the major new technologies that will be used to control offenders in institutions and the community. Identify the potential problems of each.
7. Define "the new penology" and describe its moral and practical assets and liabilities.
8. Define "accreditation" and explain why it is sought by many public and private agencies.

Chapter Outline

Introduction
The Media and the Politics of Corrections
The War on Drugs
The Costs of Rising Incarceration Rates
Changes in the Justice System
The Growing Power of Victims
New Technologies
The New Penology
Accreditation
Summary

Major Points

1. Corrections is a politically controlled system that is guided more by politics and public beliefs rather than objective reality.

2. The media presents an unrealistic image of the nature and frequency of crime in the U.S. as well as an undeservedly negative view of corrections.

3. The war on drugs is the main reason for the growing racial imbalance in U.S. prisons.

4. Rising incarceration rates may actually increase crime rates by weakening deterrence, forcing minor offenders to use violence to protect themselves, and destabilizing families and communities.

5. More people are spending more time in prison under harsher conditions as a result of tougher sentencing laws that grew out of public fear and pressure from victims' groups.

6. New technologies are making it easier to track the movements of offenders in institutions and the community but may present a threat to the liberty of all citizens.

7. Some agencies have given up efforts to rehabilitate offenders and concentrate solely on managerial efficiency; this trend is known as "the new penology."

8. Gaining accreditation with the ACA helps assure that all aspects of an agency's or institution's operations are of the highest quality.

Key Terms

ACA accreditation	New penology
Actuarial prediction	Smart cards
Agenda-setting	Victim impact statement

Chapter Highlights

Correctional systems are guided by popular beliefs about crime and other political forces. The media focus on heinous crimes and extreme cases of inefficiency have given the public a distorted view of corrections. Few reporters know much about the topic and most officials avoid the press as much as possible. The war on drugs is driven partly by media imagery and is the central factor in the increasing proportion of women and minorities in U.S. prisons. Rising incarceration rates may make the crime problem even worse by weakening deterrence and teaching minor offenders to use violence. Pressure from victims' lobby groups has contributed to new sentencing laws as well as to the growing set of new rights of victims such as impact statements and restitution. Technology developed for the military will become an increasingly important factor in corrections as corporate interest in corrections grows and military hardware become less essential because of the end of the Cold War. Lack of faith in treatment and a punishment-oriented public morality has led many correctional agencies to stress administrative efficiency as their only significant goal. Accreditation with the ACA is a traditional method of assuring efficiency and high quality in correctional agencies.

Examination Questions

Multiple Choice Items

1. Experts predict that crime will continue to _____ as correctional populations _____ over the next decade.
    a. decrease/grow*
    b. grow/decrease
    c. hold steady/decline
    d. increase/stabilize

2. Future increases in the prison population will be the result of:
    a. increasing levels of serious crime.
    b. sentencing laws passed to deal with the crime wave of the 1980s.*
    c. increased levels of domestic and foreign terrorism.
    d. new gang control laws.

3. The tough new sentencing laws used throughout the U.S. are a result of:
    a. increasing crime rates.
    b. growing levels of juvenile violence.
    c. the public's loss of faith in alternatives to imprisonment.*
    d. all of the above.

4. The media's power lies in its ability to direct the public's attention toward certain topics and away from others. This power is known as:
    a. agenda-setting.*
    b. mind control.
    c. opinion manipulation.
    d. propagandization.

5. Television news coverage of crime has _____ since 1990.
    a. decreased by 50%
    b. increased tenfold*
    c. remained stable
    d. been ignored

6. Media coverage of crime is focused on acts that are:
    a. especially heinous.
    b. very untypical.
    c. simple to explain.
    d. all of the above.*

7. Which of the following is NOT a reason that corrections receives little positive publicity?
   a. it has very few successes*
   b. its successes are undramatic
   c. former clients would suffer from publicity
   d. agencies are often prohibited from campaigning for their own interests

8. Politicians sometimes encourage the media to focus on crime in order to:
   a. strengthen support for budget increases.
   b. divert attention from other problems.
   c. promote their personal beliefs about social control.
   d. all of the above.*

9. The drug felt to be most closely linked to crimes of violence is:
   a. alcohol.*
   b. cocaine.
   c. heroin.
   d. marijuana.

10. Which of the following is an important part of the effort to make prisons tougher?
    a. charging inmates for educational programs
    b. eliminating treatment and educational programs
    c. eliminating or reducing prevention programs in the community
    d. all of the above*

11. Making treatment less available, offering no incentives to participate in it, and making life in prison harsher is expected to:
    a. reduce the crime rate through greater deterrence.
    b. increase the crime rate by worsening the amount of prisonization experienced.*
    c. reassure citizens that the government is primarily concerned with their safety.
    d. all of the above.

12. In the last decade, the powers of the police and correctional officials have:
    a. been continually reduced by the courts.
    b. been expanded by the legislatures and courts.*
    c. come to focus on prevention and treatment.
    d. remained the same.

13. As correctional populations grow and life in prison gets harsher, the problems faced by practitioners:
    a. increase in number and severity.*
    b. decrease in number and severity.
    c. remain unaffected.

14. The victims' movement and politico-religious conservatism:
    a. are strongly correlated in their content and timing.*

   b. have very different goals for the correctional system.
   c. have achieved few political successes.
   d. support crime prevention and treatment.

15. _____ allow victims to describe how the crime affected their mental, physical, and financial welfare as well as their family, job, and social relationships.

   a. Jury charges
   b. Sentencing guidelines
   c. Victim impact statements*
   d. All of the above

16. Which of the following technologies is likely to be a part of corrections in the future?

   a. reliance on computers for information storage
   b. knife resistant materials
   c. military tracking and sensing devices
   d. distance learning technologies
   e. all of the above*

17. A " _____ card" resembles a credit card but holds information describing the personal traits, security classification, and medical condition of an inmate and can be used to track offenders from jail to prison and then to parole.

   a. commissary
   b. smart*
   c. computer-linked
   d. prison ID

18. The _____ focuses on risk management and administrative efficiency rather than punishment and rehabilitation.

   a. new penology*
   b. criminal court system
   c. alternative sentencing movement
   d. all of the above

19. _____ of predicting behavior are based on factors that predict violence or recidivism for broad categories of people, such as drug or sex offenders.

   a. Anamnestic methods
   b. Scientific methods
   c. Actuarial methods*
   d. Psycho-social methods

20. _____ is guided by a commission of experts that constantly revises the standards in dozens of manuals to keep up with new court decisions and technologies.

   a. The new penology
   b. The federal prison system
   c. Modern probation
   d. ACA accreditation*

True-False Items

1. Correctional attempts to achieve efficiency and fairness are based on scientific data rather than public beliefs.
   a. True
   b. False*

2. Correctional policies are more a product of politics than the crime rate.
   a. True*
   b. False

3. The media has immense power to change the beliefs of citizens.
   a. True
   b. False*

4. Data clearly show that even low levels of drug use make otherwise normal people commit heinous crimes.
   a. True
   b. False*

5. By focusing almost exclusively on the individual offender we ignore the effects of culture on the amount and nature of crime.
   a. True*
   b. False

6. The growing tendency to reduce treatment while increasing sentence length and the rate of imprisonment is a purely political trend.
   a. True*
   b. False

7. The victims' movement is dominated by liberals who are applying their political beliefs to modern prison management.
   a. True
   b. False*

8. The new penology does not try to eliminate or reduce crime; it simply tries to improve the coordination of the social control system.
   a. True*
   b. False

9. As the Cold War becomes less important, much military technology is being adapted for use in corrections.
   a. True*
   b. False

10. ACA accreditation legally guarantees that inmate lawsuits against an agency will be dismissed.
    a. True
    b. False*

Essay and Discussion Items

1. List three major reasons why corrections is poorly represented in the media. How does this imagery affect the ability of correctional agencies to perform efficiently?

2. How is the war on drugs likely to affect correctional populations and agency priorities in the next decade?

3. Why do many experts feel that raising the rate of imprisonment is a very inefficient way to combat crime?

4. How has the growing power of victims affected the correctional mission? On what kinds of forces is the power of this movement based?

5. What effects are new technologies likely to have on corrections in the 21st century?

6. What is "the new penology" and how has it changed the priorities and goals of corrections?

7. What is "accreditation?" How is it achieved? Why is it useful?